CREDIT SCORE SECRET:

*A Complete Beginner's Guide On
How To Repair Your Credit, Improve Your Score,
And Boost Your Business.
Including How To Write A 609 Dispute Letter.*

Scott Moss

SCOTT MOSS

© Copyright 2020 - All rights reserved.

The content contained within this book may not be reproduced, duplicated or transmitted without direct written permission from the author or the publisher.

Under no circumstances will any blame or legal responsibility be held against the publisher, or author, for any damages, reparation, or monetary loss due to the information contained within this book. Either directly or indirectly.

Legal Notice:

This book is copyright protected. This book is only for personal use. You cannot amend, distribute, sell, use, quote or paraphrase any part, or the content within this book, without the consent of the author or publisher.

Disclaimer Notice:

Please note the information contained within this document is for educational and entertainment purposes only. All effort has been executed to present accurate, up to date, and reliable, complete information. No warranties of any kind are declared or implied. Readers acknowledge that the author is not engaging in the rendering of legal, financial, medical or professional advice. The content within this book has been derived from various sources. Please consult a licensed professional before attempting any techniques outlined in this book.

By reading this document, the reader agrees that under no circumstances is the author responsible for any losses, direct or indirect, which are incurred as a result of the use of information contained within this document, including, but not limited to, errors, omissions, or inaccuracies.

SCOTT MOSS

Table Of Contents

INTRODUCTION 8

CHAPTER 1: CREDIT SCORE? WHAT IS IT ABOUT? 14
- What is Credit Score? 14
- How Credit Scores Work 16
- How Credit Scores Are Created? 16
- Commonly Used Scoring Systems 20
- Credit Score Values 21
- FICO Score 8 Ranges and How Lenders View Them 22
- How Credit Scores Are Calculated 22
- Credit Report 23
- What's a Good Credit Score? 24
- How to Obtain a Good Credit Score: 26
- Why Use Different Credit Scores Instead of Just One? 31
- What you need to know if you have no credit score 33

CHAPTER 2: GET YOUR CREDIT REPORT 36
- Be careful with free credit score websites 39
- How to quickly increase your credit score 40
- More Tips on How to Increase Your Credit Score 42
- The Simple Steps to Improving Your Credit Value 44

CHAPTER 3: THE FICO SCORING MODEL 48
- Understanding FICO Credit Score 49
- What about the other three factors? What do they measure? ... 54
- How FICO Scores Help You 55

CHAPTER 4: THE DIFFERENCE BETWEEN FICO AND OTHER CREDIT SCORES 60
- Different Bureaus Use Different Models for Credit Score Calculation 60
- The Difference Between FICO and Other Credit Scores 62

CHAPTER 5: WHY IS IT SO IMPORTANT TO HAVE A GOOD CREDIT SCORE? 64
- Access to best credit cards 66
- Easy access to loan 66
- Lower interest rates on loans 67
- Easy approval for rental of houses and apartment 67
- Better job applications 68
- Negotiating Power 68

CHAPTER 6: WHAT AFFECTS MY SCORE? 70
PAYING LATE OR NOT AT ALL 70
HAVING AN ACCOUNT CHARGED OFF OR SENT TO COLLECTIONS 71
FILING BANKRUPTCY 73
CLOSING AN OLD CREDIT ACCOUNT 74
MAKING A NEW APPLICATION FOR LOAN OR CREDIT 75
DEROGATORY FINANCIAL SETTLEMENTS 75
HIGH BALANCES OR MAXED OUT CARDS 76
CLOSING CREDIT CARDS 76
NOT HAVING ENOUGH MIX ON THE REPORT 77
APPLYING FOR TOO MUCH 78

CHAPTER 7: COMMITMENT, DISCIPLINE AND THE RIGHT MINDSET WILL MAKE THE DIFFERENCE! 80
AVOIDING THE BAD CREDIT WITH THE RIGHT MINDSET 80
FEATURES OF A BAD MONEY MINDSET 81
QUALITIES OF A POSITIVE MONEY MINDSET 82
EMPLOYING A POSITIVE MONEY MINDSET TO CIRCUMVENT FINANCIAL CHALLENGES 82
FIND FINANCIAL BALANCE 83
A MONEY MANTRA 84
THE DEBT SNOWBALL METHOD 84

CHAPTER 8: CAN I RAISE MY SCORE TO 800+ POINTS? 88

CHAPTER 9: STEPS YOU CAN TAKE TO IMPROVE YOUR CREDIT SCORE BY 100+ IN 30-60 DAYS 94
PAY OFF YOUR LINES OF CREDIT & CREDIT CARDS. 95
UTILIZE YOUR CREDIT CARDS LIGHTLY 95
CONCENTRATE ON CORRECTING THE BIG MISTAKES ON YOUR CREDIT REPORTS 96
UTILIZE THE BUREAUS' ONLINE DISPUTE PROCESS 96
CHECK WHETHER YOU CAN HAVE YOUR CREDITORS UPDATE POSITIVE ACCOUNTS OR TO REPORT 97
LOOK FOR ANY ERRORS ON YOUR CREDIT REPORT 97
DISPUTE YOUR ERRORS 97
ACTIVATE AUTO-PAY ON YOUR CARDS 98

CHAPTER 10: HOW TO BUILD A CREDIT SCORE FROM SCRATCH? 100
THE FIRST IS TO OPEN A BANK ACCOUNT 100
THE SECOND IS TO APPLY FOR A SECURED CREDIT CARD 101
NEVER EXCEED 30% OF THE CREDIT CARD LIMIT 102
PAY YOUR INSTALLMENTS REGULARLY 102
VARY THE TYPES OF DEBT AS MUCH AS YOU CAN 103
ADD YOUR NAME TO SOMEONE ELSE'S CREDIT CARD AS AN "AUTHORIZED USER" 103

Download the free Credit Karma app 103
How to Grow a Good Credit Score Over Time 104

CHAPTER 11: HOW TO IMPROVE YOUR CREDIT SCORE AFTER FORECLOSURE AND BANKRUPTCY 108

Managing Foreclosure/ Bankruptcy/Tax Lien and Other Judgments 108
What is Foreclosure? 109
Now, Bankruptcy? 110
Types of Bankruptcy 113
Concerning business, the two types of bankruptcy are: 114
The Basic of Credit Card Debt and Bankruptcy 115
Implications of Bankruptcy 119
Pros 119
Cons 120
So, what can you do to maintain it? 121
Improve Credit Scores After Foreclosure 122

CHAPTER 12: HOW CAN I INCREASE MY CREDIT LIMIT? 126

Ensure your credit report is accurate and free of errors 126
Pay down your balances 128
Open new accounts 128
Increase your credit limit 129
Open a secured credit card / loan 130
Do not apply for too many things at once 130
Clear up your collections and derogatory marks 131
Fix your credit utilization ratio 131

CHAPTER 13: SHOULD YOU USE A CREDIT REPAIR COMPANY? 134

TransUnion 135
Experian 135
Equifax 135
Making the Best of Credit Bureaus 136
How the Bureaus Get Their Information 137

CONCLUSION 140

SCOTT MOSS

Introduction

Do you understand your credit score? You should. A credit score can decide your qualification for the nuts and bolts of life. Your credit rating influences your capacity to buy a home, land a decent financing cost on advances, or even find a new line of work. It speaks to the danger of non-installment that you present to a moneylender.

This book is written to provide information as accurate and reliable as possible. This book will learn all about what credit is and what you have to watch out for. You will find out how to spot negative items in your credit reports and learn about important strategies that you can employ to clean up your credit reports. Remember that you are not entirely helpless and hopeless if you have bad credit. You can repair your credit on your own.

After you have repaired your credit, you can use the tips in this book to keep your credit record clean at all times, learn about ways to rebuild your credit and work for financial freedom. These steps are not at all difficult to take. You simply have to be willing to take them.

We all want to have a nice credit rating because we understand that this makes access to credit easy and affordable; that's why we will do whatever it takes to ensure that we don't do anything that might threaten that rating. What happens when your efforts don't bear the needed result in boosting your credit rating? Credit repair might be the best solution for you. In any case, why should you pay more when you shouldn't? This book will walk you through the process of repairing your credit to ensure all negative items are removed from your credit report forever.

Nowadays, credit is extremely important given that most people use it almost every day, even without knowing, like it is a part of their daily survival. These include credit cards, house payments, and car payments, among others. Regrettably, many people fail to consider their credit rating until they run into trouble dealing with it.

When you have a bad credit rating, it can affect not only your ability to obtain a loan. It may also result in problems when securing any type of credit. For instance, you may encounter problems when renting a property, paying deposits on your phone lines, other utilities, or getting a store financing. As such, it is necessary to pay attention to your credit rating.

On the other hand, if you have a bad credit rating, there are several possible things that you can do to carry out a credit repair. The first crucial step is getting your credit report. You should know that all information regarding your credit is reported, by your bank and other financial institutions that you are involved with, to credit bureaus. In turn, the credit are the ones holding the key to start implementing repair.

More often than not, people pay little attention to their credit reports unless they are already in a situation of credit repair. You must get a copy of your credit report regardless of what your credit rating reflects.

If you are attempting to carry out a credit repair, you need to look into your credit report. There are cases wherein credit reports have inaccuracies or discrepancies. For instance, your credit information may have been confused with another individual's file whom you have the same name with. There are also cases wherein there are erroneous data on your credit file. There are many cases in which people are surprised with reports of missing payments by mistake.

Should you find any inaccuracies or discrepancies in your credit report, you can carry out a credit repair by requesting, usually in writing, that the concerned credit bureau investigate the disputed items. In your request, you may include supporting documentation, if available, or simply state your dispute and request for an investigation.

If you're struggling with poor credit because of decisions on your part or something else, we will give you some tools to restore your good name and get you back on track. Most people struggle with a negative mark on their credit from time to time but don't be fooled into thinking there is no way back. Hopefully, by the time you finish reading this book, you'll be back on the road to a viable financial future with a more positive financial image to give to the world.

Here in this book is the answer you've been looking for. A chance to reclaim your life and provide you with everything you need to start again, on the right foot.

To reestablish a bad report, all you need do is to contract a specialist credit repair organization to do it for you or do-it-without anyone's help. The do-it-without anyone else's help strategy is good for individuals that want to dive deep into the procedures and understand how the system works.. In any case, you will probably still need a guide or manual to carry out the more technical aspects.

Good credit can help you out in life, and you can make a better score happen.

You need to have the best credit score if your goal is to easily and effortlessly secure an advance. You will likewise appreciate the perks that come with it as your credit rating goes up. One of the biggest advantages of having a superior credit score is having lower scheduled installments.

You can move in the direction of a noteworthy credit score by taking care of your tabs in time and guaranteeing that you utilize close to 30% of the credit you have accessible at a given time. You ought to likewise abstain from taking an advance except when you need it. Likewise, don't be enticed to utilize different credit extensions simultaneously. Moreover, check your credit reports in any event once in a year and check for any mistakes present.

SCOTT MOSS

CHAPTER 1:

Credit Score? What is it About?

What is Credit Score?

Credit score is the number derived after analyzing a person's financial records, particularly his credit history, to determine his creditworthiness level. It is a number that represents how well that person handles all the money that he borrows. It is the main determinant used by many lending companies, next to or together with the five C's of credit (character, capacity, capital, collateral, conditions). While the latter determines the creditworthiness of a person, the former objectively interprets it.

Most companies use numerous credit assessment measures to assess their potential borrowers' creditworthiness, but the credit score stands to be the most objective of all. Credit scores help many institutions in making financial and corporate decisions. Lending companies such as credit card companies, banks, and other financial institutions use the credit score to determine the possible risks they will face when lending money to a person.

They also use this score to evaluate the possible losses they might experience due to unpaid loans and bad debts. They also use this score to determine who are qualified to be their borrowers, the amount they will lend to them, the different terms and conditions that they may impose for each of them, and the interest rate they can charge to them.

For instance, obtaining credit is a person's option whenever he runs out of cash. He can still buy using a credit card issued by the lending company. However, issuing a credit card takes many steps, one of which is assessing his financial capability. The credit score will help lending companies in determining if he is a creditworthy person.

Creditworthiness is the measure of the possibility that a person will pay his financial obligations. Other countries, however, consider creditworthiness as the measure of the possibility that a person will fail to comply with his monetary obligations.

Creditworthiness is important in financial matters because lending companies also have to generate revenue from lending money. Suppose they do not check the creditworthiness of each of their borrowers. In that case, they may find themselves in bankruptcy either because their borrowers are cashless or because they already have left the country. Creditworthiness serves as a means to protect the interest not only of the lending company, but also of the public.

How Credit Scores Work

The key to improving your credit score is understanding what it is made of and how it works. If you can break it down into its components, you can tackle each one separately. It makes it simpler to understand what is coming from where, and how best and quickest to change things for the better.

How Credit Scores Are Created?

There are several different scoring systems available today. Each one has its proprietary algorithm and approaches things differently.

Each company or entity chooses which system to use. In a few cases, they may calculate your credit score using different methods before deciding.

FICO scores are by far the most used, with over 90% of credit institutions relying on them. Data analytics company FICO (formerly Fair Isaac Corporation) does not reveal its proprietary algorithm used to calculate the final score. But it is known that the formula relies on five major components, each weighted according to importance.

But, as already stated, FICO's is not the only current score calculation system out there. There are several others. Due to differences in the calculation mechanisms used, your score may differ by 100 points across different systems.

The FICO Scoring Model

FICO holds the most reliable scoring model thanks in no small part to its longstanding track record. Fair Isaac Company began computing these scores back in 1989. They have since revised the algorithms several times in the past over three decades to adjust for shifting factors to produce continuously dependable credit scores.

The ranges in between 600 and 740 mean from average to above average credit worthiness. In 2014, FICO introduced its FICO 9 scoring model.

The primary revision in this model was to reduce the importance of unpaid medical bills. The reasoning behind this is that medical debts that are not paid are not truly financial health indicators.

You might be waiting for insurance to pay a medical bill or simply be unaware that a medical bill had been given over to a collection agency. For some people, this critical change allowed their credit score to increase by up to 25 points.

Other changes in 2017 stopped collectors from reporting late medical debts that were not yet 180 days delinquent. Year 2017 also saw the three credit reporting bureaus drop all their data on civil judgments and the tax lien records from their files. FICO reported that this helped the scores of around six percent of consumers. Before FICO 9 came out, FICO 8 (that the company developed in 2009) was the standard credit score version. FICO 8 remains the most commonly utilized score of the lending industry. FICO 8's distinguishing features were to penalize you for charging near your total credit limit each month and provide pardon if you had only a single late payment of over 30 days.

It is worth noting that each time FICO releases an updated version on its scoring models, lenders may keep the version they are using or upgrade. FICO 8 has remained the overwhelming favorite because it costs so much to upgrade to the new model.

here are lenders still using even FICO 5 models. You can ask your lender which model they are using when you go through the application process.

FICO scores typically do not change that much over the short term. The exception is if you start missing payments or showing charge offs and defaults. Not everyone has a FICO score either. If you do not have credit, you will fall into the category of what experts call "credit invisible."

You must have six months of payments reported to the credit bureaus to have a FICO score.

Many people do not realize this, but it is a federal law that allows you to view your credit reports at least once a year. It might seem strange, but there was a time when you would not have been allowed to see what information had been collected about you. The credit bureaus felt that since you would not have been their primary consumer, they were not obligated to inform you about any information collected concerning you. However, a federal law issued about 25 years ago changed all of that. Now, you can check your report from each of these agencies at least once a year.

If you have not checked your report in a long time, it is strongly advised that you check all three. If you have checked it, it is recommended that you pull from one agency once every four months to see exactly what has changed on your report and make corrections as soon as they happen. Getting a copy is pretty easy. First, go to AnnualCreditReport.com and follow the instructions for requesting your report.

Commonly Used Scoring Systems

We have already mentioned the FICO score, which is the most widely accepted score calculation method. FICO uses several different scoring models, each designed for a specific purpose. Their NextGen scoring model, for example, is used to assess consumer credit risk, while the FICO SBSS is used to evaluate small businesses applying for credit.

FICO relies on the three national credit bureaus to calculate credit scores. These are Experian, Equifax, and TransUnion. Each of these credit bureaus may have different information on any one given consumer. In a bid to outcompete FICO, these same three bureaus collaborated to produce their credit scoring system. Known as the Vantage Score, it differs from FICO in several ways. A credit report created using the Vantage Score may show significantly different values than one for which FICO was used. Although not as commonly used as FICO, Vantage Score is also well-accepted by the financial community. Some financial institutions will pull credit reports from both systems for a consumer before deciding. There are some other scoring systems available too. CE Score is published by CE analytics. Currently, this score is made available to over 6,000 lending institutions across the U.S. And frequently, financial institutions may choose to use non-traditional credit scores to gain further insight into their consumers. Most of these scores are based on data not available to the national credit bureaus. Such credit scores may rely more on utility, rental, and telecom payment data. Public record information such as mortgages, property deeds, and tax records may also come into play.

Credit Score Values

Each time your credit score is calculated, it will come up with a specific value. The range for these values depends on the scoring system used. FICO and Vantage Score 4.0 (the latest Vantage Score model) calculate a score ranging from 300 – 850. Other scoring systems have entirely different scoring ranges. In general, though, one thing remains common across all orders: the higher your score, the better for you. While no calculation model is perfect, lending institutions still view consumers with a higher rating as carrying a lower risk. It makes them more likely to offer you their services and gets you a better deal.

As FICO is the most used credit score by far, we will take a closer look at how their credit ranges are broken down. The FICO Score 9 model is the most recent, but many institutions are still using the FICO 8 model so that we will break down below.

FICO Score 8 Ranges and How Lenders View Them

SCORE RANGE	CLASSIFICATION
300-559	Poor
560-669	Fair
670-739	Good
740-799	Very Good
800-850	Excellent

How Credit Scores Are Calculated

What your credit score reads is based on the factors considered when calculating it. These will vary significantly across different scoring systems, and even across different scoring models within the same network.

As mentioned previously, FICO and Vantage Score, while using different scoring algorithms, both rely on the data from the three national credit bureaus. That is Equifax, Experian, and TransUnion. Other, less traditional scoring systems may use only some of the information available from these three credit bureaus or none. They may choose to rely on data not available from these bureaus, such as rental and utility payment histories. Public record information, such as mortgages, liens, personal property titles, and deeds, is also frequently used. Each system will use a given set of data to calculate your credit score, assigning each component weight or importance. It usually comes through as each component contributing a specific percentage toward the final score. Some elements, such as your payment history, will weigh very heavily. Other things, like new credit, will have a much lower impact. Again, this varies according to the scoring system used.

Credit Report

The main document used by lending companies in computing a person's credit score is the credit report. It contains various personal and financial information of the individual such as the place they live, the specific manner through which they pay their bills, their current financial condition (whether they are currently bankrupt or insolvent), and whether they been sued for collection of money due to unpaid loans. Obtaining a credit report is free, so before a person applies for credit, they must get a copy of it. The Fair Credit Reporting Act (FCRA), the law governing the reporting of a person's credit information, requires every credit reporting company or agency to provide a person a free copy of their credit report once every year at their request.

What's a Good Credit Score?

In the current economy, it's a lot harder to qualify for a loan. Presently you need an excellent credit score to qualify for most types of credit. So what's a good credit score rating?

850 is immaculate credit and the most elevated credit score rating conceivable; however, I've never personally observed anybody with an 850. A good credit score begins in the 670 territory. Scores lower than 670 are not viewed as good credit.

In general, credit score values range from 300 to 850. A lower value means that a person is less creditworthy, while a higher value means that he is more creditworthy. However, this interpretation is broadened by the lending companies using their respective financial data on their clients. Instead of referring to a high or a low credit score, they have developed certain brackets that explain how creditworthy a person is. The following explains what each range of credit scores mean:

a. A credit score of 751 to 800 allows a borrower to apply for credit with the lowest interest rate and the most competitive amount because the lending companies have an assurance that he will not default in his monetary obligations. Many consider this score as the best. Someone who gets a score within this range can be almost certain their application will be granted.

b. A credit score of 711 to 750 allows a borrower to apply for credit at competitive interest rates. While the person's credit standing is relatively good, a slightly higher interest rate would be charged to them compared to someone who scores 751 and up. Someone who scores at this range gets a relatively good credit standing.

c. A credit score of 651 to 710 allows a borrower to apply for credit at moderate interest rates. This is the normal score that applicants must get to ensure that their application will be granted.

d. A credit score of 581-650 may be allowed to apply for credit, but he must obtain it at high interest rates. This is because at this range, the possibility of risks and loses is getting high.

e. A credit score of 300-580 does not allow a person to apply for credit. Their application may be granted, but they can only avail it if they are willing to pay the highest interest rate. This is because at this range, possibility of losses is very high.

However, one must take note that there is no general method in determining the credit score of a person. Its computation depends on the company assessing him. His credit score may be different when assessed by different companies, but also the range of scores may be interpreted to mean the same thing because of the elements considered in assessing him.

For instance, his score may be 375 in one company and 340 in another, but both scores mean that he is less creditworthy and has to repair his credit score fast.

How to Obtain a Good Credit Score:

There are five criteria that your credit is scored upon which are rather simple to follow.

Your Payment History accounts for 35% of your credit score.

Do you pay your bills on time? If you don't do anything else yet make timely payments, you will have a good credit score in two years. Staying away from late payments is one of the most effective ways to support your credit. Otherwise your past actions will continue to harm your credit score. One ongoing multi day late payment will bring down your credit score, in all probability by 20! A few late payments and your score will drop extremely far, exceptionally fast. Being late by multiple days can hurt your score considerably more, and they are a main problem when assessing your credit score. Know that the later the wrongdoing, the more negative the impact on your score. While there is often a grace period, anything over 30 days will cause real damage to your credit score. Make sure to analyze your debt and check in with your bank statements. Be very diligent in making timely payments and deal with accounts before they are late or go to assortment. Try not to overextend yourself so that it harms your odds of making timely payments. If you have old late payments that can't be removed or fixed from your credit report, realize that time heals old injuries, and your score will increase if no new misconducts are reported. Always remember to pay before the "Grace Period" placed on your credit cards. Creditors charge extra expenses for late payments. This is an exceptionally enormous benefit for the banks. A bank may charge a $30-$35 expense for being 2 hours late on your payments! (be sure to look at the fine print on everything) Numerous banks have also introduced other feeds associated with multi-day late payments triggered even before the 30 days. Don't cut it too close with your due date. Get your payments in fast or set up automatic payments so you don't forget.

Amount Owed accounts for 30 Percent of your credit score.

The credit scoring model determines credit balance, usually against your high credit limit. This is calculated in rates. It's imperative to keep your balances as low as could be allowed. If you have a card with a $5,000 credit limit, keeping your balance beneath $500 places you in the 10% scope of accessible credit. There are thresholds in debt proportion that will make your credit score bounce higher. These thresholds are 70%, half, 30% and 10%. If you can't pay off your credit cards for the whole amount, pay them down BELOW the following conceivable edge. Calculate your credit limits along these lines. If you have a card with a $5,000 limit, increase 5000 x.10 (or .30, .50, .70) You will need to pay your balance for at least under these sums. For this situation - under $500 (or $1500, $2500 or $3500).

Keep in mind; the principal activity is to check your credit report for credit limits. If your high limit isn't reporting, the scoring model will utilize your balance as your credit limit. This implies you're utilizing 100% of your availability. Call your creditor and make sure they correct it. Conveyance of debt is a simple method to make sure you keep up a solid score.

Try to have a good spread of debt with a lower balance to limit proportion. For instance, it's better to have $2,000 debt on 5 cards than to have $10,000 on a card with all others paid off. In the case you're creeping up towards your credit limits, apply for more credit, or request an increase in credit from your current accounts.

This criterion depends on all out availability, not estimate of availability. It doesn't make a difference if you need $500 or $50,000. It's how you handle it that matters. Breaking debt onto extra cards or credit lines can assist you with raising your score rapidly.

The Length of Credit History counts for 15% of your credit score.

Length of credit history is about time the length or period you've had your credit accounts. If you've had a credit record open for 15 years, it is more stable than if you have had one for just two months. An important hint here is never to close your credit cards. Keep your old accounts open if they are in good standing, regardless of whether you don't utilize them and there's a zero balance. However, keep in mind that you need to use your credit lines a little to keep the active. Accounts unused for over 6 months become idle and are overlooked by the credit bureaus, except if there is a reprobate action joined to that record. Keeping your credit lines open likewise helps in improving your credit availability, clarified in the previous section. If you want to include credit, ask your card organization to increase your credit limit. The best way to increase your credit lines, beside getting another card, is to broaden your line on an old record with a good and long history. Be sure they report the credit amount increment to the bureaus accurately. A standard factor of amazingly good credit scores are long credit narratives. Credit reports that possess old accounts with a fifteen to twenty-year history will probably have a lot higher scores. In conclusion, it is important to add older stable credit lines to your report and keep them in good standing even when not using them.

Amount of New Credit accounts for 10 Percent of your credit score

New credit means fresh out of the box or newly opened accounts. If you have just opened your account you will need to build up its authority gradually. If you have recently applied for 10 credit cards, banks will, in general, accept the likelihood that possibly you've lost your employment and are needing a backup plan. Try to begin with one little credit extension and work from that point. Every time you start a new credit line, make sure that you can deal with the payments reliably, not be late, and keep your balances as low as is allowed, or paid off.

Kind of Credit Utilized accounts for 10% of your credit score.

The credit scoring model loves to see that you have an assortment of credit types in your file. The absolute best arrangement of credit is to have a home loan, a vehicle payment and a couple of credit cards. This credit is spread crosswise over various types of lenders and sort of credit reached out to you. There are a couple of types of credit to avoid. Payday loans are terrible to have credit with and your scores will likely be damaged for having these types of high-risk loans. Other very awful types of credit are the offers that enable you to have no payments for a year. These are hazardous, because the conditions of the understanding usually incorporate that if you don't pay the loan off in a year, on day 366 you will owe the whole years' worth of payments at normally 20% interest. This is a debacle already in the works. Individuals who more than once go for these offers are individuals who fall into credit difficulty. You ought not have that sort of credit on your credit report.

Why Use Different Credit Scores Instead of Just One?

This is a very important question with a very simple answer. There are many different credit scores out there, just like there are different cars such as pickup trucks and four-door sedans.

Imagine two cars that are about the same size and are nearly the same shape. They're hybrids that can be electrically charged or run on gasoline. They both have gears, steering wheels, comfortable seats, and four wheels. Yet, some people will go for one company's model while others will choose the other option.

People have different preferences when they select cars. It's a similar situation when it comes to credit scores. Some lenders prefer certain credit scores over the others. All credit bureaus use the information in your credit report. Still, their treatment of the information varies slightly as per certain lenders' needs, which is why there are different ranges and credit scores.

Therefore, it is important not to get too caught up in your credit score. The number has meaning for your lender and for that one transaction you'll be performing with them. The online credit scores are just a reference point for you to know how creditworthy your lender thinks you are. Taking this score to the lender, however, may not be enough to approve your loan.

They probably won't base their decision and subsequent loan on the online score you bring because they might just be using a different one than the one you brought. This may happen even if you bring the score from the same credit score developer.

A better idea would be to look at the range of the model used and see where you fall in that range. It would be in your interest to pay close attention to the risk factors statements that come with your score.

In case the lender is giving you the scores, it is a good idea to get the risk factor statements with those scores. If you have accessed the scores, you'll also get a list to see what has affected your scores the most and how they turned out.

You should tackle the issues mentioned in the risk factor statements first to be a less risky borrower. These statements will be very similar to each other regardless of the credit rating companies you used to get it. When you work on those issues, you'll be able to get better credit over time.

No one has a perfect credit score, ever, is that when you have credit you are carrying some risk, by definition. These risks will be shown in the credit scores you receive.

What you need to know if you have no credit score

Lack of information makes individuals have misbeliefs and misconceptions when it comes to issues relating to credit cards. You need to know some things to be well-informed about credit scores and what to do if you do not have a credit score.

It limits your options for credit score

For you to get credit, you need credit. Without a credit score, it makes it more difficult for you to get lenders that you can borrow from. Though it isn't impossible for you to get credit without your score, lenders need proof that you can make online payments, properly manage funds, *etc.* before they can decide to loan you. So, starting small with a student loan can help you make regular, on-time payments and build your score.

No credit score – bad credit

Not having a credit score might suggest that you've not needed a credit score, which isn't something bad. It also doesn't necessarily mean that you have a bad credit habit just as you might think.

Building a credit score takes time

To build your credit score, it means that you can repay an amount of debt over some time. This is no easy process which takes time since many factors contribute to your credit score. Once you have established a credit by obtaining a loan, you will begin to build your credit history and your credit score as soon as you pay back.

SCOTT MOSS

CHAPTER 2:

Get Your Credit Report

Finding your credit score online is easy but can also be dangerous. Hundreds of individual websites offer to check your credit quickly and usually for free, but the process itself requires you to provide extremely personal information to the sites. Sensitive personal information typically required includes your social security number, address, name, and sometimes a phone number. While these unofficial sites can potentially secure your credit score, they can sell your information and are generally not trusted.

Some of these sites are also related to identity theft. In general, you should never provide your full Social Security number online due to potential security risks. While there are dangers to finding your credit score online, there are ways to access the information securely. An essential factor to remember is that while most credit scoring sites these days offer free credit score checks, some will try to charge you. This is one red flag, and you should never pay for a credit check unless you have them all the time.

By law, you are allowed to check the top four lenders every year. Additionally, if your bill was declined on credit, you can view a denial report. The easiest way, but not the most convenient, is to contact every branch to check your credit: Experian, Equifax, TransUnion, and Innovis. A simple search allows you to find all the websites of the agencies mentioned. These agencies give you your credit score individually, but if you want a faster way to check your credit score, you can always use one of the objective credit checkers, which combine scores from three and sometimes four agencies. One of these sites is www.experian.com. Sites like Experian will also offer toll-free lines that you can use to check your credit score if you have any questions when providing information online.

However, be aware that all of the above agencies and websites will try to sell you packages and services designed to create, save, or protect your loan. While some of these services can be helpful, in general, spending and using credit responsibly is the best way to build or protect your credit score.

Knowing a person's credit rating has never been easier. Today, many online businesses are focused on providing credit reporting services. Anyone interested can search online to find the right service for their specific needs. It is true that in many ways, an individual's creditworthiness is like a brand. Many people and businesses will review this assessment and base their decision on whether or not to partner with an individual. However, what many people are not sufficiently aware of is that potential employers and colleges will also be looking through a prospective employee or student's records. A bad grade can lead a company or a school to decide not to do business with that person.

The downside of modern life is that a three-digit number can determine whether someone is considered worthy of association or not. That's why knowing your credit score is essential. With knowledge comes the ability to use that knowledge. If a person discovers that they have a low rating, they can actively improve themselves in several ways, such as debt consolidation or public debt grants and loans. In addition to a result considered "good", there are also ways to increase this number. In general, opening new credit accounts that an individual can quickly pay off over time will increase their credit score.

Be careful with free credit score websites

Hundreds of websites offer free credit scores. However, the truth is that many of these offers are not free. There are several different tips and methods by which you are tricked into parting with your hard-earned money.

The most popular websites offer a free credit report, but once you fill out many online forms, you are asked to pay a fee. Many will pay for it because they spent a lot of time filling out all the details and don't want to start repeatedly with finding another website or wasting more time.

There are other methods, when they do give access to your credit card information but then you are billed a month later for some service you didn't notice in the fine print and you have completely forgotten about it.

Now you know some things you need to pay attention to, but how can you find your credit score for free and avoid all the scam sites that seem to pop up everywhere?

While many companies and websites offer a free credit report, only a few can be trusted.

Search on Google and see how many sites there are. Look at reviews or ask around before giving your details. There are many ways to obtain credit score reports directly through the institutions, so you don't have to rely on sketchy websites.

Even when you have picked the right website, check the small print for extra services that might come up later.

How to quickly increase your credit score

There are many reasons why you may need to increase your credit score quickly. One of them is that some employers have recently started checking their potential employees' credit scores before hiring them. The reason is to ensure that employees can manage their finances and that their performance is not affected by financial difficulties. For people who are thinking of changing jobs but have lousy credit, now is the time to immediately consider taking steps to correct bad credit. Do not wait any longer.

Now the critical question is how to repair your bad credit effectively. Let me share with you some helpful steps:

Step 1: Find out your exact credit score.

Some like to assume that their credit scores are bad because they haven't made multiple payments before. This is wrong. You must know the exact credit score before you take any further action. If you want to be quick, you can check your credit score online at the AnnualCreditReport.com website. To play it safe, you should also get a credit report from one of the major credit bureaus, i.e., Experian, TransUnion, or Equifax. Once you know your credit score, you need to plan the appropriate strategies to improve it. We remind you to carefully review your credit report to make sure there are no errors. If you notice an incorrect report, you should contact your credit bureau to correct the mistake immediately.

Step 2: Collect money to pay off your past debts

No matter how bad your credit report is, it would help if you always faced it with courage. If you have past debts that you have not yet paid off, it is advisable to raise funds to pay off the debts. Don't be afraid to connect with collection agencies. Obtain their consent to remove negative entries from your report after paying your debts. If you can't pay off the debt all at once, you can negotiate with them to pay it off in installments. Never run away from debt collection agencies as this will worsen your credit rating.

Step 3: Budget to pay your monthly bills

In addition to managing your old debts, you should also keep an eye on your checking accounts. You must make your monthly payments on time. This way, you can gradually increase your credit rating.

For example, if you have a credit card in hand, you will be reminded to make sure there is no unpaid balance on your monthly statement.

The truth is that no matter how bad your credit score may seem now, there are ways and strategies to fix it. It all starts with budgeting and paying off debt.

Slowly and with the right information you will get a better handle on the situation and handle your finances with ease.

If you cannot deal with lenders to increase your credit score, it is best to seek a professional counselor who continually deals with these issues.

After a few steps, it will help you improve your credit score.

More Tips on How to Increase Your Credit Score

Achieving and maintaining a high credit rating is not that difficult. At least when you know what it does, it will become straightforward and you will wonder why you struggled with this for so long in the past. You need to do many things to get a high score, and there are some things you need to do to increase your score.

Let's see what you can start doing right now to make the most significant difference.

Tip 1 - Too Much Credit is Bad!

If you've made the mistake of opening too many credit cards and too much line of credit, you may be keeping your score low without even realizing it. Having a lot of credit available is excellent, but you never want to stretch yourself too far and negatively affect yourself. Not more than 3 to 5 revolving accounts (credit card accounts) must be opened simultaneously. You will also want to save the balance on low cards, the higher the balance, the less credit you have available which will bring the score down!

Tip 2 - Be careful with whom you have the opportunity to settle your loan!

A few years ago, I made this mistake when I authorized several car dealerships to handle my loans, and they also applied for sales cards within a few weeks. My rating was around 720, and it dropped to 680 just for all the apps I had. Every time my credit was taken, it fell like a rock! Whatever the reason, credit bureaus don't like your loan to be spent in a short period.

Tip 3 - Check Your Credit Report for Common Mistakes!

Most credit reports will contain some errors. Just go through the report and find anything that doesn't look right or is a separate error.

You will have the option to dispute the records and delete them. This will quickly increase your credit score! Many people don't realize that mistakes are always there, but few people "make mistakes". Take a look at yours, or you might miss it!

The Simple Steps to Improving Your Credit Value

1. Always pay your bills on time!

2. Live below your means!

3. Save money in your savings account for small and large purchases. If you don't need it, please don't buy it! If you want it, save it!

4. Every six months, check your credit reports for errors, inaccuracies, incorrect data, duplicates, and negative loans that are outdated. A FREE loan report can be obtained once a year online at annualcreditreport.com. If you want to check your credit reports more than once a year, you can buy them for around $9 from each credit bureau. If you get your credit reports in your annual account or at one of the credit bureaus, the results will not go down.

5. Keep your credit card balance low by about 1/3 of the limit. Never exceed this amount and never increase your credit card; it will lead to lower credit scores.

Be aware that some credit card companies reduce consumption limits for no reason and without notice above maximum credit limits.

6. Open two or three revolving credit cards at the same time. Having too many revolving credit cards open, even if your balance is zero, shows that you could go out tomorrow and increase your credit card limits. If you are closing accounts, you will want to close new ones, NOT old ones. Older people give you a higher credit score. Loan companies respect the opening period for credit card accounts. They usually require at least a year or two of on-time payment.

7. If you have your driver's license number on your driver's license, replace it with your usual computer-generated name. If you lose your driver's license, you have all the information someone needs to remove your credit identity. They can use your data to get credit, buy things online, get credit cards, etc.

If your Social Security number is deducted from your driver's license, it will also prevent auto repair shops from running credit reports without your approval. Some agents will ask you to provide a driver's license for insurance purposes. Still, they use your social security number, name, and address to write up a credit report on you and see if you have enough credit before spending more time with you.

8. Unsubscribe from pre-approved spam by calling: 1-888-303-7722

9. Don't accidentally apply for a loan or add your social security number in forms. Loan applications appear as inquiries on your credit report, signaling lenders that you may be taking on new debt. Tip: Insurance companies now ask for your social security number to make you an offer. Don't apply for a loan often (this is called a hard move); your goal here is to keep your credit reports from showing excessive demands that will hurt your credit score.

10. Lenders want to see stability. It means living in the same place for more than two years, staying in the same job/career for more than two years, etc. If you are moving often, get a mailbox to make it look more stable.

11. If you have billing accounts, agree to a lower amount (called your debt settlement). This will save you money, but keep in mind that it doesn't mean the item will be deleted from your credit report. A "paid collection" will be displayed, but it's better than an "open collection". You may perform credit repairs to remove derogatory items from your credit reports when they are paid or not. Government law, the Fair Credit Reporting Act, states in Section 611 that if an item on a credit report is inaccurate, out of date, duplicated, misleading, or cannot be verified, it must be removed or corrected.

The law says the consumer has the right to an accurate credit report. The statistics are staggering, given the number of mistakes the agency makes regarding people's credit reports.

12. Also, if collection agencies call you, you should exercise your right under the Fair Debt Collection Practices Act and ask them to "verify the debt". This will accomplish four things: 1. show that this unknown company has the right to collect the alleged debt; 2. that an unnamed company proves that the debt is valid; 3. prevent them from making annoying phone calls, and 4. prevent them from adding another negative tag to your credit report.

13. Any change in your credit report can dramatically affect your results. For example, merely closing two accounts not only reduces the number of accounts opened in slices (which will usually improve your score) but also reduce the total number of all open accounts (which generally reduce the score). Likewise, such action will affect all accounts' average age, which could increase or decrease the count. As you can see, one simple change affects a lot of items on your credit report. Therefore, it is impossible to give a 100% estimate how a particular action will affect your credit score.

CHAPTER 3:

The FICO Scoring Model

Most people do not realize that the credit bureau that issues your reports does not determine your score, another company does it, a third party called the Fair, Isaac Corporation (FICO). They weigh all the different elements of your credit report to determine what number you get. All the data collected by the credit bureaus are factored in to come up with a three-digit number.

This is probably the only grade you should seriously worry about after you get out of school. It is the grade you get for your financial stability. That single three-digit number will tell the world what they should think about you. But it is not a number that reflects only the present it is also a pathway to your future. If anything is wrong with your reports, it is your responsibility to get it fixed. This is the primary and most effective way to change it.

Thus, you must know what's in your report so that you can correct any incorrect or incomplete information. This will help to bring your score up higher. Very few people have a perfect score, but you can improve that number if you know what to do.

Understanding FICO Credit Score

FICO Scores are numerous elements almost all lenders in the U.S. think about when they settle on key credit choices. A US News and World Report article expressed that "The FICO Score is the No. 1 bit of information to decide the amount you'll pay on a loan and whether you'll get credit." Such choices incorporate whether to endorse your credit application, what credit terms to offer you, and whether to expand your credit limit once your credit account is built up. FICO Scores are utilized by many creditors, including the 50 biggest lenders, making it the most generally utilized credit score. At the point when you acknowledge new credit and oversee it tenaciously by reliably paying as agreed, you show to lenders that you don't have credit hazard. Lenders utilize your credit history as a method for assessing how well you have dealt with your credit till date.

A FICO Score is a three-digit number determined from the credit information on your credit report at a customer reporting agency (CRA) at a specific point in time. It outlines your credit report's information into a solitary number that lenders can use to survey your credit chance rapidly, reliably, unbiasedly, and fairly.

Lenders will utilize your FICO Scores to assess your credit hazard—and proceed with your application. It is also an objective measure that you obtain depending on your genuine acquiring and repayment history without being influenced by other types of information, for example, race or religion.

Your FICO Scores from every agency might be diverse because FICO Scores depend exclusively on the particular credit information in that agency's credit file. Not all lenders report to each of the three CRAs. Indeed, even in situations where the lender reports to each of the three CRAs, the result may appear different depending on the evaluation process.

Notwithstanding the three-digit number, a FICO Score incorporates "score factors" which are the top factors that make up your score. Tending to these score variables can assist you with improving your monetary wellbeing after some time. Having a good FICO Score can place you in a superior situation to qualify for credit or better terms later on.

Lenders use FICO Scores regarding a wide assortment of credit Items such as:

- Credit Cards

- Auto Loans

- Personal Loans & Lines of Credit

- Student Loans

- Home Equity Lines & Loans

- Mortgages

FICO or the Fair Isaac Company, in particular, calculates your credit score based on 5 things:

Payment History: 35%

Length of your Credit History: 15%

Type of Credit Utilized: 10%

New Credit Taken On: 10%

Amount Owed to Lenders in Total: 30%

What do these values mean? It means that some things will have a larger effect on your credit score. If you miss any payments or don't make them on time, that will change your credit score more than, say the total amount of debt you have (amount owed to lenders in total). Both of these factors have a high significance and should be taken very seriously. Another thing that is covered in the amount that you owe is your utilization. This shows the amount of debt you have taken on as compared to your available limit on credit. If 30% or more of your credit limit is utilized, it will likely negatively affect your score.

720 and Above Excellent

When you have this score, you get the best interest rates and repayment terms for all loans. This score can come in handy if you are hoping to make some major purchases. You will be able to get credit without any problems and at the lowest possible rates. But then, this score is extremely hard to establish. You will have to put in a lot of effort to maintain this score and still, you will not come anywhere close to 800. The most you can wish to come close to is 720 and remain there for as long as possible.

680-719-Good

When you are in this category, you will get good rates and terms but not as good as those with excellent scores. With this score, you can get favorable mortgage terms. You might not face as many problems but will have to be ready to run around from company to company to approve your credit. Again, this score is not very common. You need to put in extra effort to get it over the 680 mark.

If you cannot cross this limit because of some erroneous charges, you must try your best to get it cleared as soon as possible.

620-679-Average

When you are in this category, you can get fair mortgage terms and have it easy when buying smaller ticket items, (of course with no better rate than good and excellent scores). Take care not to slip down to the level where a mortgage plan is unaffordable.

580-619-Poor

When you are at this level, you only get credit on the lenders' terms. You will probably pay more to access credit so be ready for extra charges. You should also remember that you cannot access auto financing if your score goes lower than this range so you should work towards building it. This is where a large majority of individuals lie. Their score will be bad mostly owing to wrong entries. If you are here, then you will have a tough time getting credit within your budget limits and will have to be ready to pay up a lot of money.

500-579-Bad

If your credit score is in this range, access to credit will cost you dearly. If you are looking for a 30-year mortgage, you could be looking at 3% higher interest rates than how much you would pay if you had good credit. On the other hand, if you are looking for something short time like a 36-month auto loan, you will probably pay almost double the interest rate you would pay if you had good credit. So being here is probably the worst thing that can happen to your credit report. It is almost impossible to get low interest rates.

Less than 500

If your credit score goes to this level, it is so bad that it might be almost impossible to get any type of financing. If you do, the interest rate will simply be unfathomable. You might have to spend 30 to 40 years trying to repay it. Your entire life will be dedicated toward repaying a loan that is not worth it.

I am sure several of you are in this last range. But do not panic as help is at hand. You might wonder if it is possible for you to fix your score if you are in this category and the answer is yes! You can improve your credit score and possibly enter the good range.

What about the other three factors? What do they measure?

Firstly, the longer the time you have credit, the better you will be in the lender's eyes. This determines the length of your credit history.

Think of this as relevant experience on your credit value; the more you have, the higher your credit score will be. A reasonable and sizeable 15% of your credit score has been attached to your report for this reason.

Secondly, if you've applied for credit recently, it accounts for 10% of your score. Think of this as recent relevant experience—except instead of getting a good job, you get good credit. The last thing that the credit companies look for to determine your credit score is the different credit types you have. An example of this is that a person is likely to have slightly better credit than you if they have a car loan and a mortgage on their credit report along with credit cards, while yours only has credit card accounts.

How FICO Scores Help You

A FICO Score gives lenders a quick, objective and predictable gauge of your credit risk. Before using scoring, the credit allowing procedure could be moderate, conflicting, and unjustifiably one-sided. Here are a few different ways FICO Scores help you.

Get credit quicker

FICO Scores can be conveyed immediately, helping lenders accelerate credit card and loan endorsements. This implies when you apply for credit, you'll find a solution immediately, even within seconds. Indeed, even a home loan application can be endorsed a lot quicker for borrowers who score over the lender's base score necessity. FICO Scores likewise permit retail locations, web locales, and different lenders to make "moment credit" decisions. Remember that FICO Scores are just one of numerous factors lenders think about when settling on a credit decision.

Credit decisions are more attractive

Utilizing FICO Scores, lenders can concentrate on the realities identified with credit risk, instead of their genuine beliefs or inclinations. For example, factors such as sexual orientation, race, religion, nationality, and conjugal status are not considered by FICO Scores. So when a lender utilizes your FICO Score, it is assessing your credit history that is reasonable and objective.

A Higher FICO Score sets aside you cash

When you apply for credit – regardless of whether it's a credit card, a vehicle loan, an individual loan or home loan – lenders need to see how risky you are as a borrower to settle on an appropriate number. Your FICO Scores may influence not just a lender's decision to give you credit, but also how much and what rate.

Think about these two models:

Two individuals are getting $230,000 on a 30-year contract. A borrower with FICO Score of 760 could pay $211 less every month in interest in contrast to a borrower with a FICO Score of 630. That is an investment funds of $75,960 over the life of the loan.

On a $20,000, 48-month automobile loan, the borrower with a FICO Score of 720 could pay $131 less every month in interest compared to a borrower with a FICO Score of 580. That is a total of $6,288 over the life of the loan.

Many people do not realize this, but it is a federal law that allows you to view your credit reports at least once a year. It might seem strange, but there was a time when you would not have been allowed to see what information had been collected about you. The credit bureaus felt that since you would not have been their primary consumer, they were not obligated to inform you about any information collected concerning you. However, a federal law issued about 25 years ago changed all of that. Now, you can check your report from each of these agencies at least once a year.

If you have not checked your report in a long time, it is strongly advised that you check all three. If you have checked it, it is recommended that you pull from one agency once every four months to see exactly what has changed on your report and make corrections as soon as they happen. Getting a copy is pretty easy. First, go to AnnualCreditReport.com and follow the instructions for requesting your report.

SCOTT MOSS

CHAPTER 4:

The Difference Between FICO and Other Credit Scores

Different Bureaus Use Different Models for Credit Score Calculation

There are different scores that lenders can get from the different bureaus and the score for one may not mean the same thing as the other. This is important because when you get your credit score, it is imperative that you know exactly what your number means and if you're in hot water or not. There are different credit scoring ranges for different lenders. Here are the most popular ones:

a) FICO Credit Scoring Range

Extension of Range: 350-850 is the credit score range. The Fair Isaac Corporation's credit score is what many lenders see when they look at your credit report.

This score is one of the most used out there. The FICO score shows how creditworthy you are in the eyes of lenders.

There's not just one type of FICO score as new next generation/NextGen scores have been introduced that go up to 950.

b) Vantage Score Credit Scoring Range

Extension of Range: 501-990. The Vantage Score credit scoring model is formed by the 3 major credit bureaus, namely TransUnion, Equifax and Experian.

When you receive your credit score from one of these bureaus directly, they will most likely give you this Vantage Score. It is also referred to as the Vantage Score 2.0 model.

c) Vantage Scores 3.0 Credit Scoring Range

Extension of Range: 300-850. This credit scoring model is largely similar to the previous one (Vantage Score 2.0 Model). The only big difference is that the range is slightly larger for the Vantage Score 3.0 Range, i.e. 300-850.

d) Trans Risk Credit Scoring Range

Extension of Range: 300-850. This range is used by the credit bureau Trans Union when they are trying to pin your creditworthiness down.

e) Equifax Credit Scoring Range

Extension of Range: 280-850. This is the scoring range used by the credit bureau Equifax, to show how risky it is to lend to you.

f) Experian Plus Credit Scoring Range

Extension of Range: 330-830. This one is used by the credit bureau Experian and is how that credit bureau shows how creditworthy you are.

The Difference Between FICO and Other Credit Scores

Another question that you may have along the way is the differences between the FICO score and the other credit scores. To get started, these scores are the only ones created by the Fair Isaac Corporation, and they are used by about 90 percent of the top lenders when it is time to make lending decisions overall.

The reason for this is that FICO scores will be seen as the standard when it comes to making fair and accurate decisions about an individual's creditworthiness.

Now there are other credit scores out there, and they can be used in some situations. These other scores will calculate the number they give you differently than the FICO score can. So, while it may seem like some of those other scores are similar to what we see with the FICO score, they aren't. Only FICO scores will be used by most of the top lenders you want to borrow from, and while the others can be good for some monitoring of your score, if you would like, the best way to go is with the FICO score.

CHAPTER 5:

Why is it so Important to Have a Good Credit Score?

When you apply for credit, insurance, telephone service and even a place to live, providers want to know if you have a good risk level. And to make that decision, they use credit scores.

A credit score is a number. A high score means you have good credit. A low score means you have bad credit.

A higher score means that you represent a lower risk and are more likely to get the product or service - or pay less.

It works as follows: Credit managers extract information from your credit reports, such as your bill payment history, your accounts' age, your unpaid debts and the collection actions initiated against you.

Credit scores can be used in various ways. These are some examples.

1.**Insurance companies** use the information in your credit report and combine it with other factors to predict the probability that you present an insurance claim and predict the amount you could claim. They consider this information to decide if they will grant you insurance and how much they will charge you.

2.**Public service companies** use credit scores to decide if they will require a new customer deposit to provide the service. Cell phone providers and homeowners who rent homes also use scores when considering a new client or tenant.

Each type of company has different scoring systems, and credit scoring models can also be based on other information apart from your credit report's data. For example, when you apply for a mortgage loan, the system can consider the amount of the advance, the total amount of your debts and your income.

Access to best credit cards

Having a good credit score is an essential factor to qualify for an opportunity to get a credit card that provides excellent cash-back reward programs, awesome advantages, low rates and so many others. Besides paying lower interest and fees, having access to the best credit card means you can get a larger credit limit. Therefore, you can have freedom and flexibility to make purchases you want without the financial constraint that arises from a small credit limit.

An increase in your credit limit results into an increase in your creditworthiness overtime. This shows banks and other lending institutions that you are mature enough and can handle the responsibility of having access to a large amount of credit.

Having a good credit score can help you discover cards with cash-back rates as high as 5% at different places like restaurants, grocery stores, E-commerce platforms, gas stations and any other time your card is used.

Easy access to loan

Having a bad credit history will make you scared of applying for a new credit card or loan due to the fear of being turned down. Maintaining a good credit score tells a lot about your credit responsibility. When banks and lending institution see your credit score, they can be rest assured that they are not at risk and you are likely to pay back the money you are asking them to loan to you. Though this does not guarantee an outright approval because other factors such as your income, debts, etc. are also considered, it just provides you with a very good chance of getting approval.

Lower interest rates on loans

The interest rate that you get to pay is directly dependent on your credit score. Suppose you have a very good credit score. In that case, you might not need to consider the interest rate when applying for a credit card because you will always qualify for the best interest rates thereby paying very minimal charges on credit card loans. If you always want your interest rate to be low, you need to have a good credit score.

Easy approval for rental of houses and apartment

So many landlords and apartment owners tend to check credit scores for the same reason lenders do routinely. They fear that tenants with bad credit score might be unable to keep up with rent payment and avoid the hassle – they avoid tenants with a high risk. Having previous bad credit scores gives the property owner an unsettled mind that you might not be able to pay back at the stipulated time, a good credit score says otherwise.

Better job applications

This is not the only criteria considered by employers, however, so many employers access the credit history of various job seekers during their application processes especially when the job you're applying for requires handling money or accessing clients' sensitive financial information. Majority of employers believe that your ability to use credit responsibly makes you more likely to be a responsible employee.

Negotiating Power

You can get leverage to negotiate a lower interest rate on your student loan, new credit card, mortgage and others if you have a good credit score. Having a credit card with a history that doesn't have an iota of problems provides you with more bargaining power, that is needed to secure the favorable terms that you need. You therefore can carefully pick the terms that will be of great advantage to your present financial circumstance.

CHAPTER 6:

What Affects My Score?

Paying Late or Not at All

One of the worst things that you can do when it comes to your credit score is paying late on anything. About 35 percent of your score will be about your history of making payments so if you are not on time this will cause a huge drop. Consistently being late on these payments is going to cause a lot of damage to your credit score. Always pay your bills on time, especially your credit card bills.

What is even worse than paying late is not paying at all. If you decide to completely ignore your cards and other bills and not pay them at all, then you are going to be in even more trouble as well. Each month that you miss out on a payment for your credit card, you will end up with one month closer to helping your account be charged off.

If you ever want a chance to get your credit score up at all, especially if you are hoping to get it up to 800 or higher, then you have to stop the late payments. This will be a bad thing because it shows that you are not willing to pay your money back, and they are less likely to give you more money in the process.

For those struggling with making payments, whether these payments are often late, or they don't come in at all, it is time to get a budget in place. You live above your means, which is never a good sign of getting your score up to where you would like. When you can get your budget in place and start paying your debts on time, you will be able to get that credit score higher in no time.

Having an Account Charged Off or Sent to Collections

Next on the list is having your accounts charged off. When creditors are worried that you will never pay your bills for loans or credit cards, they will use a process known as charging off your accounts. A charge off means that the insurer has pretty much given up on ever hearing from you again. This does not mean that you are no longer going to hold responsibility for this debt at all. This is one of the absolute worst things out there when it comes to your credit score.

Another issue is when one of your accounts is sent off for collections. Creditors often work with debt collectors to be able to collect their payments. Collectors could send your account to collections after, but sometimes before, charging it all off. This is never a good thing, even if the account is charged off at that time, either. If you are at the point of your bills going to collections or being charged off, this means that you have not just missed one or two payments. It means that you have gone so long without paying the whole thing that the company figures they will never get it back. Either they have probably written it off as a tax break or they have sold it to a credit collection company that will be bothering you a lot in the future.

This is never a good thing. You are going to be harassed for a long time to pay back your debt. It will show other creditors that you have not just missed a few payments when things get tough. It shows them that you fell so far behind that someone else, someone who had given you money in the past, decided to give up on you in the process. This is hard to fight against and will not make a new creditor feel like they should loan you the needed money.

Filing Bankruptcy

This is a bit extreme that you should try to avoid at all costs. Bankruptcy is an extreme measure, and it will cause a lot of devastation to the score that you are working with. It is also going to be on your record for seven to ten years. It is a good idea to discuss all your alternatives with an advisor before filing for bankruptcy.

You need to do everything you can to avoid bankruptcy at all costs. It may seem like the best idea to work with. You assume that you can just walk away from all of the debt that you have and not have to worry about it ever again when you declare bankruptcy. This is not really how this whole process is going to work for you at all, though.

There are several types of bankruptcies that you can work with, but you will often need to go through and pay off as much of the debt as possible. And sometimes, this can be several years of making payments and having your wages confiscated and taken away before you can even get to the bankruptcy. You could just pay the debts for that amount of time instead or make some kind of agreement with the creditors for a lower amount if needed, and now have the black mark of the bankruptcy on your side.

Once the bankruptcy is complete, which can take some time, then a new problem will occur. You have to then focus on how you will handle the black mark on your credit report for quite a bit of time. This could be anywhere from seven to ten years. And you can bet that creditors are not going to look kindly on all that stuff. You will find that it is almost impossible to get any kind of credit or any other monetary help you need for a long time afterward. To avoid bankruptcy, you need to learn how to work with a budget and figure out the best ways to manage your money, no matter what the income is that you are working with. This is easier to manage than you may think and can help you get on a good payment schedule to deal with your debts and get them paid off. The bankruptcy seems like an easy way to get out of the debt. Still, it haunts you for many years afterward. It can make getting credit later on almost impossible, and it will not solve the underlying problem that got you into this situation.

Closing an old credit account

It has been observed that closure of old credit accounts leads to a drop on the credit score, most especially if the card has a balance. The age of your credit history is typically one of the factors used to calculate your credit scores.

There's always an average age of all your credit accounts, closing an old account will cause the average age of your account to drop thereby reducing the overall credit age you have available on your credit accounts. This pushes down your credit usage and could hurt your score.

Making a new application for loan or credit

Anytime you apply to get a loan, the financial institution will most-likely carry out a "credit application search" on your report, which has to be authorized by you before making a decision is made either to end lend you not.

This credit application search could reduce your credit score by an insignificant amount. The harm it can do to your account becomes enormous when you repeatedly make requests within a short timeframe.

You should ensure that you are in dire need of funds before applying for credit, to avoid drops on your credit score from constant checks.

Derogatory financial settlements

Declaring yourself legally bankrupt has grave implications on your credit score and can significantly harm your score. There are some other derogatory financial settlements such as tax evasions, and civil judgements, among others, that could be of harm to your credit score.

These items show that you cannot take care of your funds properly, and you are a risky individual to lend money to.

High Balances or Maxed Out Cards

You always need to take a look at the balances that you will have on your credit cards all of the time. The second most important part that comes with our credit score is the amount of debt on them, which will be measured by credit utilization. Having high balances for credit cards, relative to the credit limit you are working with, will increase credit utilization and make your credit score go down. For example, if you have a limit of $10,000 on a card, but the balance is at $9500 or higher, your score will not positively reflect this one.

You also need to make sure that you are not maxing out or going over the limit regarding our credit cards. Credit cards that are over the limit or maxed out will make the credit utilization that you have at 100 percent. This will be one of the most damaging things that you can do with your credit score. Make sure to paydown those debts as fast as possible to maintain your credit score and keep it from plummeting.

Closing Credit Cards

There are a few ways that closing your card will end up with a decrease in your credit score. First, you need to take a look at closing a card that still balances it. When you close that card, the credit limit you get to work with will end up at $0, while your balance is still going to be the same. This will make it look like you have maxed out the credit card, which will cause your score to drop a bit. If you want to close your account, you need to make sure that you pay off the balance before closing it.

Another thing to consider is what will happen when you close your old credit cards. About 15 percent of your credit score will be the length of your credit history, and longer credit histories will be better. Closing old cards, especially some of the oldest cards, will make your history seem like it is a lot shorter than it is. Even if you do not use the card anymore, and there are no annual fees, you should keep the card open because you are losing nothing and gaining more.

And finally, we need to be careful about closing cards that have available credit. If you have more than one credit card to work with, some that have balanced and some without, then closing the cards that do not have a balance will increase the credit utilization. You can just keep those all out of the way and see your credit report go up.

Not Having Enough Mix on the Report

While this is not as big of a deal as some of the other options, you will find that having a good mix of credit will be about 10 percent of your credit score at the time. If you have a report that only has one or two things on it, such as either credit cards or loans, it is likely the score you are working with will be affected somehow.

The more you can mix up your accounts and get them to have many different things on them, the better. You don't want to overextend yourself, but having a mix of loans, mortgage, credit cards, and more, that you pay off each month without fail, is going to be one of the best ways that you can raise your credit score without causing harm or paying too much in the process.

This does not mean that you should go out and apply for many different things all at once to get your mix up. This is something that often happens; naturally, the longer you work on your credit score. You may have a few credit cards, and then you take out a loan for a car and pay it off. Maybe you need a loan for a vacation or some home improvement, so you will have those accounts and then get a mortgage.

As time goes on, these different loans and credit amounts will come and go, but they will all show up in the credit mix and help increase your score. If you try and increase your mix all at once, you will bring up some red flags against your credit, which can cause issues as well. Doing this over a few years is the best way to make sure that your credit score goes up.

Applying for Too Much

Another thing that is going to count on your report is the credit inquiries. These will take up about 10 percent of the score that you work with. Making several applications for loans and credit in a short amount of time will cause a big drop in your credit score along the way. Always keep the applications for credit to a minimum, so this doesn't harm you along the way.

In some cases, this is not going to harm you too much. For example, if you have a good credit score and you want to apply for a mortgage, you will want to apply for a few mortgages and shop around a bit. If you do these close together, it will not be seen as bad because the lender will assume this is what you are doing, rather than you taking on too much or that you have been turned down. You can also explain this to them easily if they ask. For most other cases, though, this is not going to be a good sign. Having all of those inquiries on your score will slightly lower it, at least for the short term. And when other lenders see that you are applying for a lot of credit, they will assume that you are getting rejected. They will wonder why or they will assume that you are taking on too much credit that you will not handle, and they will not want to lend you any money either. These are just a few of the different things that you are going to work with when the time comes to handle your credit report. Sometimes the things that can harm your score are going to be much more important than the things that can help improve the score. Working on both is going to be important when it all comes down to it as well, and knowing how to avoid some of the common things that can ruin your credit in no time is imperative to getting that score up and seeing it work the way that you want.

CHAPTER 7:

Commitment, Discipline and the Right Mindset will Make the Difference!

Avoiding the Bad credit with the right mindset

A perspective towards money is an overarching mentality you have about your finances. It influences the way you make important financial choices every day.

It will significantly affect your potential to attain your goals. If you shift your perspective on income, you continue to make smarter choices on how problems can be solved.

The influence of constructive thought does indeed apply in this situation.

Features of a bad money mindset

Your attitude towards money is like moral fatigue-it pushes you to act.

If you have a positive mentality about finances, you are more likely to be confident and take the measures you need to take to be effective.

On the other hand, negativity is generating emotions which prevent action:

- Fear or intimidation
- Defeatism
- Procrastination

It's harder to see the way ahead as you shift your attitude towards money and concentrate on the benefits of what you should achieve.

A fresh outlook on money will help you easily reach your goals. So how do you build a positive mentality around money?

Qualities of a positive money mindset

Once you accept financial positivity, you begin to understand that no issue is impossible. This will be done whether you have $5,000 in interest, or $50,000. Your credit score may be 500 but no loan limit would last forever.

When you have a good attitude about your finances, you start searching for possibilities instead of seeing roadblocks and realize that any financial problem is fixable.

The secret to success is to resolve negative feelings, to concentrate on the optimistic.

Employing a positive money mindset to circumvent financial challenges

Positivity may be tough to cultivate while you are in a stressful position, but it is important.

Let's assume you have those above $50,000 credit card debt issue. There are probably several factors which drive your negativity:

• The total monthly contributions are about $1,250 and the budget is close

• But despite spending too much, the balances never seem to drop

- High interest rates currently make up approximately 60% of every investment you make

- Therefore, if you adhere to the minimal contributions it would take more than 40 years to recover everything you owe.

The first step to paying off debt and changing your financial behaviors is to adjust the way you think about income. By reflecting on what debt-free life would feel like, gaining financial security, and getting the freedom to invest your money on the stuff you enjoy most, remaining focused and meeting your financial objectives is much simpler.

Your strategic emphasis needs to be on seeking alternatives. You're not the first one to slip into debt so fast. Start from what you know: Minimal payments will not create an impact sufficiently, so you need a better plan. If you just repay the bills at $1,250 instead of meeting the full payment plan the condition changes significantly. It will only take 62 months, instead of 502 months to meet the payout deadline. In reality, five years is a fair amount of time needed for a debt repayment strategy.

Find Financial Balance

Attitude is not the only component of a positive financial mindset. You need harmony too. Stability is what fosters harmony in your financial existence.

When you invest all the energy working on debt retirement, you won't have the money available in case of a disaster. Or if you're wasting the whole day today concentrating on the schedule, you can't properly save for retirement.

A money mantra lets you have a financial target at the forefront of your mind, making taking steps simpler to produce the outcomes you like. Now let's take a peek at how to build a great personal finance mantra.

A money mantra

A money motto is a clear statement of what you intend to do in your financial existence. This can either push you to make financially good decisions or discourage you from making poor ones. Its function is to remind you and give you assurance in your everyday life. You state what you wish to manifest, and you are encouraged to behave through the act of having the idea in mind. Start by dreaming about a particular financial target you would like to accomplish during the next six months.

The Debt Snowball Method

The debt snowball approach is a debt management technique where you pay off debt in proportion from smallest to highest, gathering traction when each balance is taken out. Once the smallest loan is taken off in full, the interest you owe on the loan will be transferred into the next smallest balance.

It works as mentioned below:

Step I

List your debts from smallest to largest regardless of the interest rate.

Step II

Minimum payments should be made on your all debts besides the smallest ones.

Step III

Pay as much as possible on the smallest debt of yours.

Step IV

Repeat until each debt is paid in full.

Illustration of the Debt Snowball

Suppose you have four debts:

$500 medical bill—$50 payment

$2,500 credit card debt—$63 payment

$7,000 car loan—$135 payment

$10,000 student loan—$96 payment

Following the form of debt reduction, you will be paying small contributions on anything but the hospital bill. But let's imagine you get an additional $500 a month because you've taken a side work to cut back your costs to the absolute minimum. If you spend it on the hospital bill $550 a month (the cost of $50 plus the remaining $500), the interest will go free in one month. You would then take the $550 freed-up next month to strike the credit card balance, charging $613 in sum ($550 plus the minimum amount of $63). This way you'll say goodbye to your credit card in just four months. You make it pay off!

Now hit the auto loan to the amount of $748 a month in the nose. It'll head off into the sunset within 10 months. You are all on track! You will add $844 a month against it by *the* time you hit the student loan — which is the main liability. That means that it will be also paid in just about 12 months. Today's choices that you make will affect tomorrow. And make yourself wise.

SCOTT MOSS

CHAPTER 8:

Can I raise My Score to 800+ Points?

Now it is time for the hard part. Maybe you have been doing some of the work that we go through in this guidebook, and you have seen a nice increase in the amount of your FICO score.

This is always good news, but now we want to see further if we can get our score to 800 or higher. Only the elite have this kind of score. It is hard to get it because it requires a perfect balance of credit types, a high credit limit, and no missed payments, among other things. But it is possible.

When you can get your credit to be this high, it is a lot easier for you to go through and actually get credit and loans at any time you would like. If something happens and you have many medical bills to deal with, then this credit score can help you take care of that. It can also be used for non-emergencies as well like if you would like to start a business, get a new house, or do something else along the same lines.

So, how do you make sure that you are able to get your credit score up to 800 or higher? The first thing is to know the facts. Once you are able to answer the main question of "What is a perfect credit score?" you will find that it is easier to take on the right steps in order to figure out exactly what you can do to reach the perfect score. First, though, you need to make sure you know where you stand on the FICO scale.

Once a year, you can get a free annual credit report from any of the country's top credit bureaus, all three of them. If you go through this and find any issues on any of them (sometimes a mistake will show up on one and not on the others), then this is the time to fix them. You will never get to an 800+ score if there are a bunch of errors in your report.

The next thing that you can focus on is establishing a long history of credit.

Most of the time, with a few exceptions, lenders are going to view borrowers with short histories of credit as riskier to work with. To reach a credit score that is 800 or higher, you have to establish, and then also maintain a long history. So even if you are not using some of the accounts, keeping them open will help you to get that score up.

As we have mentioned a bit before, you need to make sure that all of your bills are paid on time. There isn't a single person who has an 800+ credit score who also has a missed payment, or a bunch of missed payments, on their report. Paying your bills late or not paying the bills at all is going to decrease your score. If you have trouble remembering the due dates, then consider signing up so for automatic payments and have that taken care of for you.

You also need to take the time to redefine your credit card usage. About 30 percent of the score you have will consist of the utilization rate for your credit, which is going to be the amount of debt you owe divided by the total credit available. Typically, we want to stay under 30 percent, but if you are trying to get a higher score, then staying under 10 percent is best.

One thing that we have not talked about much in this guidebook yet but will help you to get that higher score you want, is to learn how to diversify the accounts that you are holding onto. This is one of the best ways to strengthen your credit, and while it can take some time to accomplish this, you will find it is a great way for us to make sure your credit score is able to go up.

You can make your credit score stronger when you are able to diversify your accounts. This is not an excuse to go out there and open up 10 different card accounts at a time. What it means is that you should have a mix of different types of credit, such as an auto loan, a student loan, a mortgage, and a credit card. Ten credit cards are not going to be a diverse mix of debt or show responsibility with your score. But having a bunch of different accounts, even if some of them have been paid off, is going to be a much better option to work with.

While you work on your credit score, you need to make sure that you cut your spending and create a budget that you are able to stick with. This helps you to stay within means that you can afford and makes it less likely that you are going to fall into trouble with your spending. Although it is true that your credit is not going to factor in your income, living within your means, no matter what that number is, is a great way to raise your score.

Next on the list is to find ways that you can limit the liability that you are dealing with. When you go to co-sign a loan, remember that this may seem like a nice thing to do, but you are really taking on a risk for another person. If you do this for someone who is not able to manage their debt all that well, it is going to negatively affect your score because you will be responsible for that debt as well. If you want to make sure that you can get a credit score that is 800+, and maintain that, then it is a good idea to avoid cosigning at all.

In addition to this, you should make sure that your liability is limited in other manners as well. You should always report cards that have been lost or stolen right away. If you don't do this, then it is likely that you will be liable for any of the purchases that are not authorized at the time. And if you are not able to afford those purchases, then your score is going to be the thing that suffers here.

And finally, you need to make sure that you are restricting the hard inquiries that happen to your report. Whether it is you or another agency or institution who is pulling out the credit report and asking for a copy of it, you are dealing with an inquiry. A soft inquiry can happen on occasion, and it is generally not going to be enough to make any changes to your credit. This soft inquiry is going to happen when one of the following occurs:

You go through and do a check on your own credit report.

You give an employer you may work with in the future permission to go through and check your credit.

You have the financial institutions that you do business with go through and check your credit.

You get a credit card offer that has been preapproved, and that specific company goes through and checks your credit.

While the soft inquiry is not going to do all that much to your credit scores, you do need to be careful about the hard inquiry. This is going to be the one that is able to affect your credit score. This is when a company pulls up your credit report after you apply for a product like a credit card or a mortgage. You want to make sure that you can limit the hard inquiries as much as possible to get the best results with this.

CHAPTER 9:

Steps You Can Take to Improve Your Credit Score by 100+ in 30-60 Days

Rebuilding your credit can sometimes be an excruciatingly slow process, yet you can take a couple of accessible routes that may increase your score in as little as a month or two, as talked about in the accompanying segments.

Pay Off Your Lines of Credit & Credit Cards.

Probably the fastest approach to support a score is to lower your debt use proportion, the distinction between the amounts of revolving credit that is accessible to you and the amount that you're utilizing. One straightforward approach to improve your proportion is to redistribute your debt. In the event that you have a high balance on one card, for instance, you could transfer a portion of the debt to different cards. It's usually better for your scores to have little balances on a number of cards than a big balance on a single card.

Utilize Your Credit Cards Lightly

A significant difference between your balances and your limits is what the scoring formula likes to see, and it doesn't really care whether you pay off your balances in full each month or carry them from month to month. What makes a difference is the amount of your credit limits you're really utilizing at any point intime. You can support your score by paying off the card in full a couple of days before the deadline closes.

For example, if the bills is usually sent out on the 25th, you can check your balance online about 7 days prior and pay off whatever is owed, plus extra to cover charges that may appear before the 25th.

When the bills are really printed, their balances are pretty close to zero.(In the event that you utilize this method, simply make sure you make a second payment after your announcement shows up if your balance isn't already zero.

That will make sure you don't get damaged with late charges and indeed, that can occur, despite of the fact that you made a payment before the end of the month.)

Concentrate on Correcting the Big Mistakes on Your Credit Reports

If another person's bankruptcy, collections, or charge-offs are showing up on your report, you will need to work on having those removed.

If an account you closed is reported as open, then again, you'll probably need to correct it. Having an account filed as "closed" on your file can't support your score and will hurt it.

Utilize the Bureaus' Online Dispute Process

Some people say they get faster results when following the online dispute process.

Either way you'll have to make printouts of your correspondence and everything you have sent out.

Check whether You Can Have Your Creditors Update Positive Accounts or to Report

Not all creditors report to every one of the three bureaus, and some don't report reliably. If you can get a creditor to report an account that is in good standing; however, you may see a quick knock in your score.

Look for Any Errors on Your Credit Report

You might wonder what the difference is between a credit score and a credit report. Well, a credit report is a report that contains every piece of data used to determine what your credit score is. That being said, there can be mistakes when calculating your score. It has been known that about 21% of people have errors on a minimum of one of their reports. This means almost a quarter of people with credit scores are suffering from a lower score due to errors.

Dispute Your Errors

When you want to dispute an item, you will have to write to the credit reporting agency, telling them that you want to dispute an item, or more than one item found in your credit report. It is crucial that you include the reason you are disputing.

Once done, your request should be sent in a letter through certified mail. It is also essential to request a return receipt. This ensures that the credit agency in question has received your dispute. Make sure you maintain copies of any letters that you send, as well as the items you attach. Doing this obligates the credit reporting agency to investigate and check if your dispute holds water. This typically happens over 30 days.

Activate Auto-pay on Your Cards

It does not matter if you make use of an actual calendar stuck to your wall or if you use your smartphone's app to set an alert, you should do whatever you can to be reminded when payments on your credit cards have to be made. Ensure that you pay more than the minimum consistently. When you consider that the most significant determinants of your credit score are your payment history and the size of your debt, it makes sense to pay as much as you possibly can towards your debt.

CHAPTER 10:

How to Build a Credit Score From Scratch?

There are several ways and all of them are effective.

The first is to open a bank account

Having an account open in itself will not increase your score, but it will give you a starting point to show regular income. After a few months, you can ask your bank (remember to show off your best smile) what services they offer to increase your Credit Score. My bank, for example, offers a mini loan of $ 500 tied up to be returned in 6 months. It means that you deposit $ 500, they re-loan them to you at a favorable rate and when, in 6 months, you finish paying the installments, they give you back the $ 500. Practically in 6 months, you paid interest as a "tax" with the sole purpose of accumulating points. To put it in simpler words: from 500 and 500 you return, then you pay 500 in installments + interest and you return 500 at the end. It is an expense, but this type of loan guarantees you a considerable accumulation of points, but only if you are regular in payments.

The second is to apply for a Secured Credit Card

Unlike traditional credit cards, you do not have to show any kind of entry to get approval, but you also have a usage limit. The only thing required is a deposit which is returned to you after a year of regular use. Until a couple of years ago, the deposit was around 200 euros, but with the debt problems that developed after the recession, all the major credit companies have lowered the costs. For example, I applied with Capital One (but there are many others like Discover). The deposit was only $ 49, and the card limit was $ 200 a month with the option of 2% cash back on gas or restaurant expenses. I started using it regularly every month ONLY for these two things and, after a year, my Credit Score was already considered very good, they also returned the deposit and the cash back and the credit limit rose to 500 dollars after only six months. Of course you are not obliged to use it only for these things, but I have limited myself for two reasons.

The first is to accumulate cash back (i.e. a refund) at the end of the year. The second is to make sure I never use more than 30% of the card limit. Which brings me to the next point.

Never exceed 30% of the credit card limit

Believe it or not, it is essential that you show that you do not need a credit card to pay for your things, but that you use it only when strictly necessary or as an optional choice.

The more you use it constantly the better, but judiciously.

Pay your installments regularly

All the above points have absolutely no value if you are not constant in payments. No one here scales your loan or credit card debts from your salary. It is your responsibility to remember when you have to pay or set up an automatic payment from your bank account. I decided to set up automatic payments.

Even if your memory is excellent, you never know what can happen that can distract you and cause you to forget the due date. So I strongly suggest you do the same because even one missed payment will negatively affect your score.

Vary the types of debt as much as you can

If you can make the Secured Card And the mini loan with the bank at the same time, do it. The more options you have, the faster your Credit Score will grow. Of course, always keep in mind that if you don't pay on time, this will have the exact opposite effect and your credit score will plummet before it even had a chance to grow. So if you're not sure you can do better, don't risk it and wait a little longer.

Add your name to someone else's credit card as an "authorized user"

If, for example, you are married to an American who has had more time than you to accumulate a decent score (as in my case), it might be a good idea for him to indicate you as an authorized user of his credit cards. This does not mean that you will actually have to use his credit cards, but the more his score improves, the more he will positively influence yours. Be careful though! If you go down, he comes down with you. This type of choice involves a large demonstration of trust so be careful not to betray it.

Download the free Credit Karma app

Not only does it constantly give you a detailed report of your score, but also what has positively or negatively influenced it, which credit cards or loans are best suited to your situation, your progress, and many other functions. It's all free and, although not updated to the minute, rather accurate. It does not lower your Credit Score and also offers you many other services such as online and free tax returns. Due to Credit Karma, other major credit companies have also had to adjust to offer the Credit Score free check. For example, Capital One and Discover have now integrated this service into their offers (although in a more limited way).

If you follow these tips in a year you can afford to ask for a car loan without having to pay disproportionate interest or even more, depending on your income and your general receivables/payables situation. This reminds me of how important it is to start as soon as possible. Remember that this is the first thing they look at when you need to apply for a loan!

How to Grow a Good Credit Score Over Time

Once you've begun to climb your way out a bad credit score, the most important factor then becomes growing your score. Of course, making your payments on time is a great way to balance your previously negative activity, but there are other, more creative ways in which you can achieve this same result.

Let's take a look at the ways in which you can grow your credit in the eyes of a lender.

Negotiate Outstanding Balances

Let's say that you have a debt that ultimately had to go to a collection agency because you refused to pay the debt back within a timely manner. Of course, the debt that you owe is going to reveal itself as a negative on your credit report, but if a collection agency is involved you have the opportunity to change somewhat the way in which this debt is perceived. This requires negotiation skills. By going to the collection agency and negotiating a deal where you only end up paying a portion of your debt instead of the full amount, you look responsible. Additionally, your credit report will show that your outstanding debt has been settled, and this will help to improve your score. Other tips include making sure to put the agreement in writing, stating exactly how much you are agreeing to pay.

Pay Your Bills Twice Per Month

Let's say that you've had a particularly grueling month in terms of unanticipated bills and expenses. To compensate for this, you've decided to spend close to your credit limit. Your credit limit is four thousand dollars, and this month you have already spent three thousand. This situation is not the worst for you, because you know that you have the funds and are planning to pay off the full amount of your debt by the end of the month. Instead, you should consider making multiple payments throughout the month. This way, you will be able to reduce the amount of debt that the credit card company sees. It will seem more like you simply reallocated your funds in a certain way, instead of making it seem like you are maxing out a card and are having trouble financially. This tactic should especially be considered if you own other credit cards that are close to being maxed out or are maxed out in their entirety.

Increase Your Credit Limit

If you are not in the position to paydown high outstanding balances that exist on your credit cards currently at this time, another good option is to request an increase on your credit limit. Especially if you have recently gotten a raise, this could be a great option for you. As we discussed before, having low utilization is key to maintaining a good credit score. By opening up more credit for yourself, it looks like you are using less credit compared to the current credit that is available to you. While this will serve to grow your credit successfully, it can be risky if your spending habits are less than conservative.

You need to make sure that you're not going to immediately spend more of your credit once the credit company has extended it for you. If you have a feeling that this might be a result of a credit extension, seek out one of the other options that were presented in this chapter. Similar to a gambling addiction, sometimes it can seem like spending credit card money creates a thrill because the necessity to pay back the funds is not immediate. If you are finding that you have a hard time resisting the urge to spend large amount of money on your credit card, you might have a credit card addiction. If you notice that you are frequently maxing out your credit card on purchases that are frivolous or unnecessary, you may need to seek help. Even if you don't see yourself as a complete credit card addict, seeking financial counseling might help you save money. Saving money can also help grow your credit score because the money that you save is money that is not being spent in ways in which cannot be paid back. To put it more broadly, learning how to be financially responsible will help you to grow your credit. Knowing what to save and how to save it, as well as learning how to properly manage your funds are techniques that can be aided by hiring a financial advisor.

CHAPTER 11:

How to Improve your Credit Score After Foreclosure and Bankruptcy

Managing Foreclosure/ Bankruptcy/Tax Lien and Other Judgments.

First, what are the public records you can expect on your credit profile? Three kinds of horrible public records used to be displayed on a credit record. But not anymore. You may have heard and wild guesses about this, but straight from the horse's mouth, only one kind of public record is displayed in a credit report: Bankruptcy. But before we jump into that, you need to know that bankruptcy, even though it is the only record displayed on your profile, is not the only one to worry about. Foreclosure is equally crucial. We will start with that, and then we will see how to handle the records on your profile. Here we go:

What is Foreclosure?

Foreclosure is used to describe an official situation where a lender takes control of the asset which was indicated as collateral while applying for a loan. This means foreclosure occurs when a debtor takes over property or assets to sell when the lender doesn't pay back the money borrowed.

Though foreclosure does nothing on your credit profile, you obviously need to avoid it at all costs. Whatever you used as collateral must be something of considerable value to you. Probably your house (mortgage), your parcels of land, or a vehicle you need for work or family duties. It hurts to see those things go.

Foreclosure is a long and arduous process too. It may span up to 700 days. So, even lenders try to avoid it if they can. Foreclosure usually takes place in different formats. Some are called Judicial, others Non-Judicial. The fundamental difference is that judicial foreclosure requires the lender to obtain official consent from the court before auctioning the property or seizing it. In Non-Judicial cases, the lender is not required to obtain court permissions. They can simply seize their assets.

Just like every other loan, the easiest way to avoid foreclosure is to pay your loans on time.

Now, Bankruptcy?

Bankruptcy is a financial declaration that a person is no longer capable of paying the debts he has acquired. It is a court proven declaration that a debtor has exhausted all means of getting the funds they owed and failed. And now, all creditors will have to be lenient with them. In some way, it sounds like a method of getting relief from your debts, if not all, some.

The introduction of bankruptcy laws came after a long time when lenders could be stigmatized for life, forced into slavery or pash them down to their children.

In our days, when you declared bankruptcy, you are required to declare all of your assets. For example, if you declare bankruptcy with an outstanding of $80,000 you will state all of your personal items and assets from your house, including chairs, dresses, and artwork. It is then the job of the creditor to decide whether some of those items hold value, and can be sold, seized or not. As it turns out, many people often lose more than they were hoping to when they declare bankruptcy, and it becomes a win-win situation for creditors.

Debtors of course realize this before it's too late. This is why many attempt to mess with the records and give false statements or declarations to conceal their assets. These acts are considered Bankruptcy Fraud and are heavily frowned upon in the US. If you are declaring bankruptcy, be set to face the full complications.

Bankruptcy is filed in a situation where a debtor declares that she is entirely incapable of paying further loans. She has tried all other methods, and she is left with no choice than to seek leniency from the court.

When this is approved, the debtor declares the total assets and they are liquidated, in other words, sold to cover whatever it could of the loans. Afterward, the debtor is completely absolved of further payments. The only problem is that it reflects on your credit score for ten consecutive years. This means that every potential creditor can understand that you have been in a financial mess at some point, and you had to give things which do not measure up to the value of the loan. That is never a good sign, and singularly, it will be the reason you might not be able to get a loan for the first years after.

Bankruptcy is declared in situations where a debtor is confident that he could pay the debts but considering his current financial situation, they would need a long period to pay. This time could span into several years. In the end, a repayment plan is approved by the court, and the debtor pays over that period. He is absolved of the debt after payments. Bankruptcy reflects on your credit report for seven years. It faces a lot of criticism, and it could be a reason you're turned down too, but less likely.

Only an organization or individual that is unable to completely honor its financial obligation or make payment to its creditor files for bankruptcy. This goes to say that a bankruptcy filing is a legal course of action taken by a company or person to relieve themselves from debt obligations where all outstanding debt of the company is evaluated and paid from the company's assets. As legal proceeding goes, bankruptcy is carried out to give individuals and businesses freedom from debt they have already incurred and at the same time provide creditors with the opportunity to get their debts paid. It can be said to allow for a fresh start by forgiving debts that cannot be paid and at the same time offering creditors a substantive opportunity to get methods of repayment based on the available assets of a person or business that can be liquidated.

Theoretically, this can mean that the ability to file for bankruptcy can benefit a whole economy by giving businesses and individuals a second chance to have the utmost access to consumer credit and by providing creditors with a reliable measure of debt repayment. Once the bankruptcy proceeding is successfully completed, the debtor is to be relieved of their obligation from the debt that has been incurred before filing for bankruptcy. However, it will be on their credit record that such a person has acquired debts before and filed for bankruptcy. This information is going to remain on the record for about seven to ten years depending on the type of bankruptcy filed.

Types of Bankruptcy

There are two types of bankruptcy.

Debt Discharge

This is simply the cancellation of debt, thanks to bankruptcy. Based on the Internal Revenue Code, a debtor must add into their gross income, the discharge of indebtedness after which a court must have discharged his/her debt upon meeting all conditions.

However, if a debtor should refuse financial counseling, commits a crime, fail to fully explain the loss of his/her assets, provide false information during court proceedings or basically disobey the orders of the court, a judge can rightfully refuse to discharge the debt of such a person.

The Payment Plan

This is a kind of bankruptcy filed, where a debtor and his/her lawyer submit to the court, a kind of repayment plan of how the debtor plans to pay off his/her debts in three to five years. This plan is dependent on the debtor's income, food, and utilities, tax, and healthcare expenses.

Should the court approve the plan, the debtor proceeds to make the payments required as stipulated in the plan. If such a debtor is consistent with the payments, the remaining debts at the end of the three to five-year period will be discharged. The payments are made to a trustee from the bankruptcy court that then proceeds to pay the creditors while getting a commission too.

Concerning business, the two types of bankruptcy are:

Reorganization Bankruptcy

This is a kind of bankruptcy filed which is meant to help business owners who have serious issues with their business but still have regular income and valuable assets, reorganize the business. The business is allowed to continue its operations with the court's supervision of course.

The creditors aren't allowed to interfere with the debtors during the supervision. Business owners will have to share their reorganization plan with the creditors and provide them with part of the payment. But if the creditors do not agree with the plan, they have the right to file a competing plan.

Farming Bankruptcy

It is a type of bankruptcy specially designed for farmers of the same family. It is to help the family reorganize their farming business as well as settle all their debts.

The unpredictable nature of farming and seasonal trends are factors that are seriously considered.

The Basic of Credit Card Debt and Bankruptcy

People know the basics about credit cards. Once you are approved, you then receive your card and activate it. You can use it for pretty much anything, such as for purchasing groceries, clothing, or for paying bills.

The nice part is that you only have to make the minimum payment every month to keep yourself out of credit card debt. Unfortunately, it is this kind of thinking that often leads people into credit card debt.

Below are some basic points that most people don't realize about credit card debt.

Know when short-term loans make more sense

Sometimes we need to get some cash or find a way to pay a few bills quickly. Many people turn to credit cards for these reasons. They receive their approval within minutes and their card will arrive in the mail in about five to seven business days. However, sometimes it is better to go to your bank and talk to a loan advisor instead. If you need a couple thousand dollars to pay off your medical bills so they aren't sent to a collection agency, it might be best to take out a short-term loan from your local bank or credit union.

Credit card debt can result in bad credit

Paying off your credit cards in a less than a timely manner or missing the minimum payment aren't the only things that are going to result in your having bad credit; having credit cards that hold high balances can also increase your chances of bad credit. This is why it is important never to max out your credit cards. You should make sure you always have at least 30 percent of your credit limit available.

While it is almost impossible in today's world, your best chance of keeping yourself from having bad credit is by remaining as free of debt as you possibly can.

Owing is the easy part, the hard part is paying credit cards back

The reality of life is that you never really know what is going to happen. You could have a job for a couple of decades and then find out that you are randomly laid off due to cutbacks. You could have an illness spike that causes surgery.

There are a lot of situations that can cause you to miss credit card payments and not be able to cover your bills.

You could also find yourself struggling to pay the full minimum balance, so you may decide to pay about half of it every month.

You will find yourself spending more than you make

It doesn't matter how responsible you are with credit cards; one of the biggest reasons people find themselves in credit card debt is because they spend more than they make every month.

Credit cards are very tempting because they provide you with the thought that you can just pay it back later or make smaller payments on the purchase every month.

Although, in reality, you should never spend more than what your monthly income is.

Most people use credit cards to handle emergencies

It is common for people to tell others that a credit card is only used for emergencies, but do you keep in mind what a true emergency is? Most people live paycheck to paycheck. Therefore, when they see their checking account balance drop low and there are several days before their next payday, they will start to think about each purchase they make and wonder if they should use their credit card as it is considered an emergency or a need. The best step for you to take is to start slowly saving a part of your check and place it into an emergency fund account.

People think as long as they make the minimum payment they will be fine

In reality, you always want to make sure you pay more than the minimum payment. Think of it this way: if you have a $75 minimum payment, at least 25 percent of what you pay is going to go toward interest and fees. This means that you are only putting 75 percent of your payment toward paying off your debt. Depending on how you much you owe, this could be a low amount. If you aren't careful, you could find yourself going over your credit limit, which means your credit card company will charge you their over-the-limit fee.

Furthermore, only paying the minimum payment is going to take you years to pay off. It really doesn't matter how low you feel your credit limit is versus how high you believe your minimum monthly payment is. It can still take at least a couple of years to pay off your debt, providing you stop using your credit card.

Implications of Bankruptcy

Before you consider filing for bankruptcy, you first need to understand how it works as well as the pros and cons. It's not a simple issue that can be done quickly but has a complex side only a bankruptcy attorney understands. It would be best if you find out everything you can before filing for bankruptcy. Find below the consequences of filing a bankruptcy.

Pros

Discharge: Getting debts discharged is one major reason people file for bankruptcy. And when such debt is discharged, erasing all your debts as well as preventing creditors from collecting further payments from you, the debtor becomes relieved. It's one huge advantage of filing for bankruptcy. Not everyone who filed for debt discharge is granted. If you owe debts on alimony, tax liabilities or child support, filing for bankruptcy would be a waste of time. Such debts are not forgiven nor discharged.

Automatic Stay: Here is another advantage to be enjoyed when a bankruptcy is filed. It is a situation whereby the person who files for bankruptcy becomes automatically protected from the creditors, as well as the property over the collection of debts. The protection stays until the court finally decrees the debts to be honored and forgiven or discharged. In a situation that involves divorce proceedings, the automatic stay might be lifted.

Cons

Loss of Property: There's a possibility that a bankruptcy filer might lose his property if the court decides it's valuable enough to pay off the debt owed. This would happen if you include your property in your case to the bankruptcy trustee. Your creditor would have higher leverage in trying to get your property especially if you used such property initially as collateral.

Credit Score: Another downside to filing for bankruptcy is that it decreases your credit score. Loaners will only see you as risky when they check your credit history because filing for bankruptcy won't in any way clean up your debt history even though your debt is canceled. However, it's a better option than acquiring debt. You can always rebuild your credit score later.

Privacy: If you're sensitive about your privacy, filing for bankruptcy might not be for you, and this explains why you must do your research if you want to file for bankruptcy.

You can either prepare yourself against the consequences or look for other options. When you file a bankruptcy case, every detail about your financial statements becomes public. In other words, anyone can access your personal information without your permission. The amount you owed, who your creditors were, and your bankruptcy schedule can be assessed easily by anyone. This can be quite a bid deal if you value your privacy.

So, what can you do to maintain it?

Prevention has always been better than cure. But if you are here already, it doesn't help to keep musing over the error you've made. Pick yourself up and be set to make a better impression in future endeavors.

Try to pay other debts promptly. The more you perform better in other debts, the higher your chances of weakening the effects of bankruptcy on your profile.

Building Not Activities Passivity

This may not be explicitly mentioned anywhere, but it is just common sense. Increasing assets increases reliability. If you have sufficient resources, you will be able to mortgage them for credit. So creditors will give you credit for getting a good guarantee in exchange for their risk.

Avoid construction liabilities like credit card bills as it will affect your rating negatively.

Keep in touch with credit institutions

Always be truthful about your financial situation and be in good terms with them. Always keep in touch with them and express your inability to pay, if that is the case, and see if it is possible to make an agreement in any way. After all, they want their money and not the rating to fall.

Improve Credit Scores After Foreclosure

Foreclosure can drop a consumer's credit scores with a huge margin. If you have had the misfortune of going through a foreclosure, then the following article will tell you how to rebuild your credit score.

A fall in house prices, the subsequent recession, and the high unemployment rate has caused a number of people to default on their mortgage payments. Bankruptcies and foreclosures followed as a result of defaulting on capital and interest on home loans. Since the consumer payment history is one of the most important factors affecting the calculation of credit scores, a foreclosure obviously had a negative impact on the credit rating of all those that lost their houses. Hence, the topic of improving credit scores after the foreclosure has taken on great significance.

A creditor can initiate the foreclosure procedure and complete the entire process outside the court system, assuming that the mortgage deed has a sales clause power. In the absence of a sales clause power, the lender has no choice but to take the borrower to court. In other words, judicial foreclosure is expected. Regardless of the nature of the proceedings, the details are listed in the public record and the consumer's credit report. The information remains firmly positioned in the consumer's credit report for a period of 7 years. As mentioned above, the consumer's credit score decreases from 350 to 400 points following a foreclosure sale. Although a spotted credit report and a low credit score is a double whammy, a number of creditors give proper credit to the consumer's efforts to improve credit scores. Good credit scores are a must to procure loans at a favorable interest rate, for availing insurance, and for the sake of applying for jobs that require the applicant to assume managerial and financial responsibilities.

Improve post-foreclosure credit score

In order to improve credit scores after foreclosure, you should avail either installment or revolving credit and make it a practice to pay interest on a regular basis. Establishing a history of regular payments can go a long way in helping the consumer build his / her credit scores. The same approach can be adopted by a consumer who is interested in improving credit scores after bankruptcy.

Guaranteed credit cards

People can opt for secured credit cards to rebuild credit since consumers can be approved for these cards within 6 months of a foreclosure sale or discharge failure. These credit cards are guaranteed by a CD which acts as a guarantee for credit card companies. The credit line is usually 50 to 100% of the deposit amount. A practice of repaying the entire balance on the credit card on a monthly basis will result in the credit card company extending further credit lines to the consumer without further deposits as collateral. A secured credit card is converted into an unsecured credit card within 18 months, assuming that the consumer is careful with payments.

FHA secured loans

People whose homes have been foreclosed are required to wait for 3 years from the date of a foreclosure sale to avail themselves of an FHA insured loan. Assuming that the consumer is approved for a secured credit card and brings his / her credit score up to 620 points, FHA secured loans can become the springboard for further improvement in credit scores. The Federal Housing Administration (FHA) offers secured government mortgages that protect the lender in the event that the homeowner's default values on the mortgage. Thus, the consumer can take advantage of a down mortgage by paying only 3.5 percent of the home purchase price.

These measures are not only useful for consumers who are interested in improving credit scores after foreclosure, but also essential for people who are eager to improve their credit rating after debt settlement since a debt settlement does not completely cancel out information from the consumer credit report. The net result is a good credit report and satisfactory credit scores.

Anytime you apply for one of these services with bad credit, you end up paying a deposit. This makes moving into a new place more expensive because you need deposits for all your bills. Fixing your credit means a higher credit score, which can help you avoid these deposits.

CHAPTER 12:

How Can I increase my Credit Limit?

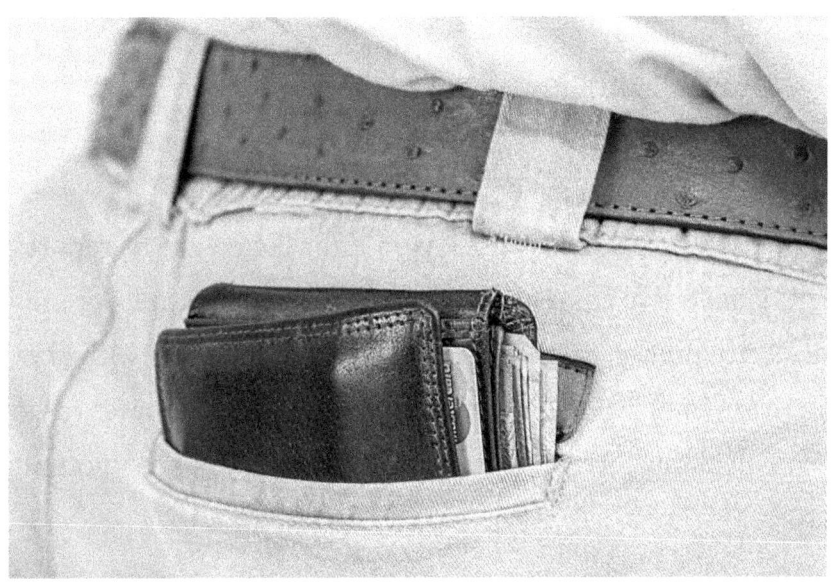

Ensure your credit report is accurate and free of errors

First check your credit reports! We each have three credit reports. These include TransUnion, Equifax, and Experian. Credit reports are not always perfect, and many of them can have errors. Up to 1/5 of people have an error on at least one of their credit reports. There are multiple ways to check your credit score. Under the Fair Credit Reporting Act, you are entitled to one free credit report a year from all three major credit report agencies. Below there is a list of some websites you can use to check your credit for free:

☐ www.creditkarma.com

☐ www.freecreditreport.com

☐ www.experian.com

☐ www.annualcreditreport.com

Some credit card companies even offer a free credit report as well. I have a credit card with Capital One that allows me to check my credit for free since I have an account with them. There are many things to keep an eye one when it comes to your credit accuracy. Here is a list of questions to spot potential errors.

◆ Is all my personal information accurate?

◆ Are all my credit accounts being reported?

◆ Are there any missed or late payments referenced that you actually paid on time?

◆ Are there any accounts or applications that you don't recognize?

Simply be sure to check for the accuracy of the information on your report. Keeping a clean report is key for a great credit score.

Pay down your balances

The amount of money you owe accounts for 30% of your credit report. Paying down your balances will definitely increase your credit score, but it is not something that's going to change it overnight. The key here is to be patient. Most people think that when you pay off a balance that it should boost your score immediately. That is simply not the case. It usually takes around 30 days or longer to see the improvement.

Open new accounts

Now, wildly applying for a bunch of different credit cards is not the strategy here. Make sure that you are in a position to open a new account. Credit Karma is great for this. CK suggests new credit cards you can apply for — based on your current credit score — along with showing you the respective approval odds for acquiring them. With this, you can limit the risks of being denied and hurting your credit even worse, since applying for credit and being denied is a black mark on your credit. If you do get rejected, however, don't fear. This will only slightly decrease your credit score. That is why it's important to be aware of your score, to know if you have a good chance to be approved for a new card or loan. Having more accounts will give your credit report diversity. Which is good! The more types of credit that you show you are responsible with, the higher your score will be. But you must be careful! Be sure to stay on top of all your payments.

Increase your credit limit

Usually if you have poor credit, you get whatever you deposit for your credit limit. For instance, if someone applies for a secured credit card and they are approved, there is usually a deposit that is required. How much they pay in as a deposit, such as $300, will be their initial credit limit. After a while, of course, you will want to buy more expensive things. You will not want to have a low limit, because it will be a lot easier to max out the card. Which is a major problem for credit. Apply for an increase in credit after you have been responsible and made all of your payments on time with a current credit card. Below you will find some tips for a credit limit increase.

☞ Pick an existing card you already have for the limit increase.

☞ Do not be greedy, only ask for a reasonable increase to show that you are responsible and understand credit.

☞ Plead your case, but don't seem needy. Apply with confidence if you have been paying on time, utilizing the correct amount of credit, your income has increased, or you've always paid the minimum balance.

☛ Wait for the right time to ask. I would recommend waiting about 4–6 months before asking for a limit increase. In those months, you must be sure you are using your loans responsibly. Credit issuers will usually review accounts every 6 months. In fact, people in good standing will usually get a higher limit increase without even asking.

Open a secured credit card / loan

As mentioned above, secured credit cards are great for people trying to build or rebuild their credit. A secured credit card is pretty much the same as a regular credit card. The difference with secured credit cards is that they require a cash collateral deposit, which then becomes the line of credit for the account. If you have had trouble getting approved for an unsecured credit card in the past, then the secured card may be right for you. Secured loans work this way as well. Many banks and credit unions offer these types of loans. They are an excellent tool to build your credit.

Do not apply for too many things at once

If you decide to apply for a credit card, wait a good amount of time before applying for another one. Problems can occur if you try to use a lot of credit at once. This can make you seem desperate and in need of a lot of money. Many stores offer in-store credit and will give you a discount for signing up. This can hurt your score if you are not prepared!

These store credits will give you a "hard inquiry" on your credit score, which could negatively impact it if you are not approved. If you get denied, try working on improving your score before applying elsewhere. A good amount of time to space out credit applications would be 3–6 months.

Clear up your collections and derogatory marks

Contact debt collectors to see if they would be willing to stop reporting to the credit agency in exchange for a payment arrangement. Normally, debt collectors will settle for less than the total amount if you speak to them and form an agreement. If you have a lot of damage, it may be hard to recover. But paying down your balances will improve your score. Also, once balances are paid off in full, most credit companies will remove bad marks from your report. Which will increase the chances of you receiving new credit and bringing your score up.

Fix your credit utilization ratio

Let's say you have a credit card, and the limit is $10,000 If you were to spend $5,000 on something, that would leave you with a credit utilization of 50%. If you were to spend the entire $10,000 on something, on the other hand, that leaves you with a 100% credit utilization. Get the picture? Many people simply do not realize the importance of staying under the correct ratio.

The key figure to remember is ***30%***! This is the ideal number to stay under with your credit limits. If your limit is $10,000, only spend up to $3,000. If your limit is $200, do not spend more than $60. Simply multiply your credit limit by 0.3 and you'll find your number. Be sure always to try to stay under that 30% for the best credit score.

These 8 tips will provide you the knowledge that you need to take your life back. Do not delay when making these decisions. Your credit is extremely important, and these 8 tips can help you improve it before you know it!

CHAPTER 13:

Should You Use a Credit Repair Company?

The best way to manage your credit responsibly is to get the right financial education and know what is best for you. This will take some time and require you put in the work to learn how everything works. Yet, since your credit scores are so crucial to dealing with your accounts and setting aside cash, you must know as much as you can regarding the credit bureaus that formulate credit appraisals. To assist you with getting started here are key details regarding TransUnion, Experian and Equifax, the primary credit bureaus of the U.S.:

TransUnion

TransUnion has workplaces nationwide that manage various parts of credit: identity theft, credit management, and other credit issues; and types of credit customers, for example, personal, business, and press inquiries. If you discover errors on your TransUnion credit report, you can call them at 800.916.8800 or visit their site to debate them. If you believe that you are a casualty of identity theft, call them at 800.680.7289 at the earliest opportunity.

Experian

Like other credit bureaus, Experian provides a wide range of various administrations for people, businesses, and the media. Experian is based in Costa Mesa, CA, and has a website. If you discover errors in your report or need to report potential identity theft, this credit bureau makes it harder to find them through a phoneline. Instead, they encourage guests to utilize online forms for questions, identity theft reports, and different issues.

Equifax

Based in Atlanta, GA, Equifax has various departments to help people with multiple types of questions and concerns. Their website is additionally set up to have people utilize online forms to work on errors, report identity theft, and handle different matters. In any case, if somebody believes that their identity has been stolen, the individual in question can, call 888.397.3742 to report it to Equifax. If you detect an error you can also go through their phone line to get someone that can fix it for you.

These are the three credit bureaus in the nation, and they each adopt different strategies to enable people to get in touch with them to pose inquiries or address any issues they might be encountering. Rather than reaching the credit bureaus directly, some people prefer to utilize a credit checking administration to assist them with dealing with their credit and stay on top of their funds. The credit bureaus all have related projects; however, most people prefer to utilize an independent organization to assist them with these issues. That way, they get an impartial perspective on their credit score and a lot more services to manage and improve their credit ratings proactively.

Making the Best of Credit Bureaus

It is important to learn that all three credit bureaus have sensitive financial data. However, there is no method to prevent lenders and collection entities from sharing your information with the above companies. You can limit any possible problems associated with the credit bureaus by evaluating your credit reports annually and acting immediately in case you notice some errors. It is also good to monitor your credit cards and other open credit products to ensure that no one is misusing the accounts. If you have a card that you do not often use, sign up for alerts on that card so that you get notified if any transactions happen, and regularly review statements for your active tickets. Next, if you notice any signs of fraud or theft, you can choose to place a credit freeze with the three credit bureaus and be diligent in tracking the activity of your credit card in the future.

How the Bureaus Get Their Information

To learn how the score gets calculated, first, we need to learn about all the different inputs of your score, aka where the bureaus get their info. You may have many factors that report information to the credit bureaus or none. Credit cards are called revolving accounts or revolving debt by the credit bureaus. Each month payments and balances are reported, as well as any late payments. This means that any cards that have your name on them will also report to all the bureaus. This includes cards that belong to a spouse or parent. If you are an authorized user on the account, it gets reported on your credit no matter what. Many people have their credit ruined by a spouse or parent going into bankruptcy or not paying their credit card bills. If your name is on any credit card that belongs to people that may not pay their bills, ask them to take your name off immediately! Installment loans also report information to the credit bureaus. If you went down to your local Sears and financed a washer/dryer set by putting up a down payment, that is an installment loan. The details of these loans are all reported; the total balance, as well as the timeliness and amounts of your monthly payments. If you have mortgages or student loans, that information does get reported. Total amounts due, total paid so far, and the status of monthly payments is all reported. This information is kept track of and organized in their databases.

SCOTT MOSS

Conclusion

Thank you again for purchasing this book! I hope this book was able to help you with your needs and to satisfy your questions regarding credit scores.

Now, you have the information that will help you build better credit and increase your credit score. Some of these strategies may not work for your situation or if you have already been employing them. Hopefully, you found a few new strategies to try and will be able to achieve the status you wish to have in your credit scores.

For those who have suffered a financial setback such as years in arrears or a bankruptcy, it will take time. It takes 10 years for bankruptcy to leave your credit history and no longer affect you, regardless of whether someone provides you with good credit lines until then. It could take 10 years for you to get back up into the 800s if you had a bankruptcy and some will not make it because they are not utilizing credit building options as stated in this book.

Anyone who has not nourished a long history with numerous types of credit may also be having trouble gaining a score above 800. However, you have fewer steps to take to get your credit scores higher. You simply need to be paying attention to the credit types you have, ensuring that you open new accounts, keep old accounts open, and establish a long history with consistent and reliable payments, as well as a small "amount owed" in comparison to your income and credit limits.

It is possible for you to have a decent credit score, or more than decent, if you are willing to work towards it. Utilize family to start to gain new credit lines, if necessary. Make certain that if you are paying for something that uses credit to build your score, by putting the funds in your account, you are going home and paying that purchase off right away. It is only the steady, reliable, and consistent credit history that is going to offer a "great credit" appearance, as well as the higher scores.

Since you have the tools available to you now, there is no better time than to get started right away with building great credit and increasing those scores.

As I have shown throughout this book, even a credit repair with a moderate success can bring you countless benefits. All that matters is that you make the time to try. If you go through this process and clear some issues you only need to repeat it in a few years. You already know what to look for and have some experience in how to think and to approach creditors and credit report agencies. The benefits of credit repairing might reveal themselves over an extended period of time but by carefully doing all the steps described in this book you will eventually clear your credit and increase your chances of you ending up with increased scores on a credit application. It will also help you with finding a job, even though your credit is not entirely repaired. When someone is evaluating your credit report and sees the written statements and all the work you have put in the process, it shows how responsible and diligent you are about your finances and says a lot about who you are.

I hope that this book has not only convinced you about the benefits that come with repairing your credit, but also that it has provided a simple and clear explanation of the steps you have to follow in order to do it successfully. I wanted to make credit repair accessible to everyone and suggest the best approach for a different number of problems. Many people become enthusiastic about credit repairing and when they see the effort involved and the time required on the journey to good credit, they get discouraged and give up. Others give up after the first negative response from a creditor or credit report agency and some even go through with it but stop doing things to improve their credit when they've finished the process and still haven't managed to fix all the negative items. Damage control is just as important as the process itself and, as I have said in the section of the book dedicated to this subject, it has many future benefits. The important thing about the whole process is to stay motivated and continue improving.

So, what is next for you? The next step is to begin applying what you have learned in this eBook in your current situation and working as hard as you can to begin repairing your credit. What have you got to lose? If you merely take a step every day, you are closer to your goal every day than you were before. It's like anything else in life; you get out what you put in. All the best to you!

Established business credit also adds value to the business. Any potential future sale of the business will be greatly benefited when the business has an already established positive business credit profile.

The stronger the profile, and more depth there is in trade lines, the more valuable the business becomes to investors and other parties who might be interested in purchasing the business in the future.

A good business credit profile and score can be built much faster than a business owner can build their personal credit profile. And business credit approvals tend to be higher dollar amounts than business owners see through personal credit approvals.

Credit limits on business credit accounts tend to be higher. It is easier and faster to get approved with multiple credit sources.

And it is easier to get approved for multiple credit cards or credit lines with individual business credit sources than it is with consumer credit approvals.

These are only some of the significant number of benefits that building business credit provides to a business and the business owner. For all these reasons, it is tough for any business to truly be successful without establishing a good business credit profile and score and leveraging that to help the business prosper.

You are now empowered with the knowledge and tools you need to ensure your business can obtain and maintain an excellent business credit profile and score. Put your knowledge to use today and get started on building business credit for your business or using business credit to help you start a new business venture.

Once you have built a positive business credit profile, you can finally have the positive business credit and financial future you deserve.

CPSIA information can be obtained
at www.ICGtesting.com
Printed in the USA
LVHW020456120221
679113LV00013B/429